To A.

with ,

from

Madeline Macdonald

3rd June 2000

THE LAST YEAR
OF
THE GANG

THE LAST YEAR
OF
THE GANG

Madeline Macdonald

The Book Guild Ltd
Sussex, England

Every attempt has been made to trace copyright holders of photographs. Our apologies to those we have been unable to find.

The Book Guild Ltd.
25 High Street,
Lewes, Sussex

First published 2000
© Madeline Macdonald 2000

Set in Times
Typesetting by
Acorn Bookwork, Salisbury, Wiltshire

Printed in Great Britain by
Bookcraft (Bath) Ltd, Avon

A catalogue record for this book is
available from the British Library

ISBN 1 85776 437 4

CONTENTS

ACKNOWLEDGEMENTS

To the many friends and members of my family who have read the manuscript of *The Last Year of the Gang* I should like to express my sincere thanks for all their helpful comments and, in some cases, for the details they provided which were missing from my own recollections. They include Elizabeth Candy, Headmistress of the Lady Eleanor Holles School since 1981; Ruby Davies, our retired teacher of history and religious knowledge; and old school friends Pamela Symonds (Pam Fish, still 'best friend' fifty years on); Trish White, named in the Diary as classmate Pat Bush, later to become Deputy Head of the school; Colleen Gardener and Hilary Symm.

My heartfelt thanks as well to Mr Michael Ratcliffe, the present owner of 7 Wolsey Road, not only for his friendly encouragement but also for allowing the use of photographs of the house as it is today.

I am also especially grateful to Mrs Alison Tramschek of Orkney who took such a kind interest in the work of the complete stranger she had met only briefly on holiday, offered many helpful suggestions and then increased my readership north of the border by passing on the book to her friend, Mrs Joan Dickson of Glasgow, to whom I was even more of a stranger!

Members of my immediate family and several of my extended family (which grows more numerous every year) have looked through the manuscript and their reactions to it have sometimes surprised me! All their comments, however, even if unflattering, were welcome and interesting.

More than anyone, however, it is my husband I wish to thank because, despite the fact that this is not the sort of book he would choose to read, he has studied it thoroughly, criticised honestly and supported me throughout the two years of my working on it.

'We three' 1950

1

THE ATOM AGE

My young sister and I, aged nine and thirteen, were convinced that the dread year 1950 would usher in the Atom Age. Hewn in granite, as it seemed, the great numbers loomed before us, while from the hollow of the future some deep gong announced our entry into the second half of a century.

We named it the Atom Age because we were both old enough to remember the war and the atom bomb and because few people at that time would have counted on World War Three being held off for much longer – rather the reverse in fact. Two great conflicts within a lifetime had put paid to the notion that any war, however huge, could 'end all wars'. It was the destiny of the entire twentieth century to be war-ridden and the stances of the major powers were doing nothing to contradict this perception. Even in childhood, therefore, this was the flavour of the Fifties: fear of war. Meanwhile, everything which later came to be called nuclear, with the derivative terms 'nuclear war', 'nuclear disarmament' and so forth, was still on the whole in those days 'atomic' or, more colloquially, just 'atom' – the atom bomb. The Atom Age.

For a brief moment at the beginning of the year it looked as if cataclysmic forces were indeed at work, but it was our mother who felt them. Diary entry: *Monday 2nd January Ceiling in sitting room came down about 6 a.m. Colonel Gettins helped Mummy clear up.* The sitting room was where she slept and the loss of precious holiday sleeping time meant an inauspicious start to the year for her, Atom Age or no Atom Age. But that, I'm afraid, was as far as it went. Within a day or two, someone called Smithy, who I think was the gardener and

1

odd job man, started coming round to repair the ceiling; and even though he had to make several visits to do the job, I don't feel the incident could be stretched into signifying the end of the world.

It was later on during that same day, however, that I must have decided it was worth keeping a record of these awe-inspiring times, for I was able to write: *Went shopping. Bought this diary*, and that is how this story began. Whether I had really planned to buy a diary or whether it was done on impulse, I do not remember, but the latter is probable because the diary is such an attractive little book that I know I'd have spotted it and wanted it. It is a 'Willowflex' diary published by Henry Ling Ltd at the Dorset Press, Dorchester. It is the size of a small prayer book, about 2½ by 4 inches in size, half an inch thick, bound in dark blue soft, hammered leather with blue print in a simple sans serif typeface. The price pencilled in by the shop was 3/1, three shillings and a penny, rather a large sum for me to spend so perhaps I had some Christmas gift money to spare. At any rate, the desire to fill blank pages with writing was as strong in me then as it is now and the little blue diary, so compact and satisfying to hold, commanded my faithful attention right through to the end of the year. As we moved into 1951, I began a new diary but I tried to make do using only an exercise book and soon, without the authority of the little blue book, it fizzled out.

Needless to say, the diary was private. *This diary is private* I wrote on the flyleaf. *The first diary I kept, to record the events as they happened each day in the year 1950, I being 13–14 years old. Madeline Appleby.* At the end of the year I wrote a poem in the back cover, again stressing the diary's privacy even though nothing of a seriously secret nature had been entered in it.

> *Whoso in this book shall pry*
> *Takes a daring liberty!*
> *With pen and paper I have said*
> *The very thoughts that cross my head.*
> *Whoso in this book shall pry*

2

Sees the events of a year gone by.
Each as it happened every day,
My only record to prove what I say.
Whoso in this book shall chance
Sees my life with every glance.
M.V.A.
Dec. 31, 1950

Decidedly intended as more of an invitation than an inter-dict, I would say. No diarist writes such a thing unless he expects somebody to read it one day. Anyhow, fifty years later, the Diary, like a state document, is being released for publica-tion and anyone who wishes can pry into it.

* * * * *

The gigantic stride into the new era which we had taken on the very first day of the year had shown little sign of dread happenings. It is recorded baldly enough: *Nan and Gag came to lunch, went home at 4 p.m. Paul came to tea and stayed to telivi-sion, Bertram Mill's circus at Olimpia.* (And at this point I need to explain that the spellings and grammar are almost all as in the original Diary and I shall leave them so in this narrative for honesty's sake, without inserting [sic] throughout the text, even where I have been careless over a name, and even though the mistakes do my thirteen-year-old self no credit.)

Nan and Gag were Nanny and Gaga, our maternal grand-parents. The strange name 'Gaga' had been my babyish corruption of Grandpa and for some reason it was allowed to remain, although my speech was generally carefully corrected. We pronounced it Gagga with a short *a* and I assume that the term ga-ga meaning mad or half-witted was not then widely used, for it never occurred to any of us in the family that Gaga might be an odd or unfortunate nickname. For the avoidance of ridicule, however, I shall spell it Gagga in this chronicle.

As for Nan, I think she herself chose to be called Nanny in preference to Grandma or Granny. For one thing, she had to be distinguished from our paternal 'Granny' on the Appleby side, and for another, in our family, confusion with the nurse-maid sort of nanny was unlikely to arise.

The two of them, Nan and Gag, lived on the border of Hayes and Hillingdon, in Middlesex; Mr and Mrs Jones they were, in a house called Cambria, making Gagga's origins quite plain to see. For the first seven years of my life we too had lived in Hayes, much of the time actually with Nan and Gag, both in the year I was born and then again following the separation of my parents.

Gagga would be 70 at the end of 1950 but was still working and in fact was enjoying what was probably the most secure job of his life as the secretary of Hayes Cottage Hospital. He had also become the Registrar of Births, Marriages and Deaths at Uxbridge Registry Office.

* * * * *

There is no reference in the Diary to its being New Year's Day nor to our having marked New Year's Eve in any way the day before. A year later, the last day of 1950 also passes without comment except for my personal satisfaction at having completed the Diary, while in the printed lists of national holidays at the front of the diary itself, New Year's Day is shown as a Bank Holiday applying only to Scotland. I believe people sometimes observed a tradition of seeing the New Year in, perhaps in the night clubs of London, but it cannot have been universal enough for me to notice that we missed it. I simply know that somehow, when I was older, I gleaned the knowledge that my mother disliked the New Year and would never have wished to join in any celebrations anyway. The thought of it saddened her.

Our First of January, therefore, simply followed a pattern similar to that of any other day in the Christmas holiday, and Nan and Gag might have come over simply because it was a Sunday. The other visitor, Paul, was from the house next door. He was a cheery, open, amenable little boy of about the same age as my sister Jan (Janice), that is, probably nine at the beginning of the year. Though the youngest of three, Paul was

4

more like an only child, the long gap between himself and the older brother and sister being due to the death of a little girl who'd come before him. He was gregarious, though, and from the time of our first meeting in 1946 he had throw himself more eagerly than most of the other local children into our games. He caught on to the spirit of our fantasies, frequently sharing with us some new source of inspiration, from a film or book,

Paul and Jan

for the schemes and adventures we enacted. At an early stage in our comradeship with Paul we appointed him Fourth Head of the Gang, the highest position left open to him, as Chris, our cousin in Hayes, was Third Head.

Other children we mixed with included the three Fermor sisters with the attractive names of Tina (Christine), Sorrel and Lorianne, from further along our road, and from opposite us the Bellears, brother and sister Jennifer and Richard. Tina was six months younger than me but more mature and less inclined to want to 'play', while the two smaller Fermor girls were much the youngest in the group. Jenny Bellears was eleven or twelve and Richard about as old as Jan and Paul. All were nominally members of the Gang, but only loosely attached.

This was the time, anyway, when I was gradually being forced to face the fact that the days of the Gang and its adventures were ending. I clung on, having these other, younger children around me, hoping I suppose to perpetuate the strange imaginary world in which we had played for so long, but 1950 would be the last year of the Gang.

* * * * *

5

The house we lived in was number 7 Wolsey Road in East Molesey, near Hampton Court. Colonel Gettins (who had been on hand so promptly to help Mummy clear up the ceiling) and

Colonel Gettins

Mrs Gettins were our landlords and lived in the main part of the house above us. I look back upon the Colonel as perfectly fitting the role life had put him in. With his fine white moustache, he looked exactly as an elderly Colonel ought to look and his background was just what it ought to have been to produce an English officer and gentleman: Harrow and the army in India. Until writing this narrative, however, I had never sought to find out more about him and did not fully appreciate his attainments. Let me now, therefore, introduce him with his correct rank and give a brief account of his career. He was Lieutenant Colonel Joseph Holmes Gettins, OBE, a man with an impressive record in the field of education, both in civilian and army life. At the turn of the century he had been Professor of Education at the University of Reading. He won the DSO in the First World War, and by 1921 he had become Chief Education Officer at Sandhurst. Ultimately he was Commandant at the Army School of Education at Shorncliffe and it was at the end of this term of service that he was awarded the OBE.

Sorrow lay in his past. His first young wife had died in the great influenza epidemic at the end of the First World War and he had returned home from the fighting one day too late to see her alive. He had met the widow who became *our* Mrs Gettins many years later.

In retirement by the time we knew him, in his late seventies I suppose, he worked in the garden a great deal (and even with the assistance of Smithy it would have been a serious occupa-

6

tion to run the large garden at Number 7) and pursued the scholarly interests which his classical education had given him. He marched with the British Legion each year on 11th November. I can see now that he was perhaps a lonely man.

Kathleen Winifred Gettins was about 20 years younger than the Colonel. She still led an energetic academic life and travelled as often as she could, chafing at the post-war restrictions over currency. (I remember her once declaring that if she could not take all the cash she required on one of her trips, she was going to smuggle a couple of diamonds into France by sewing them into the little elasticated sections of her swimming costume.) Her marriage to the Colonel had been openly an arrangement for companionship and convenience on both sides and as such it was probably very successful. But he spent time alone in the quietness of his study while the household and tenants, including we two children, whirled about him. He was to us a benign but rather remote presence and he was never Uncle Joe in the way Mrs G. was Auntie Kathleen to us from the beginning.

Kathleen Gettins had taken a First in English Literature at Somerville, probably during or just after the Great War. By the time we came to know her she was in her fifties and was occupied in two main professional spheres: as a lecturer at the Central School of Speech and Drama and as a writer. She had in the 1920s and '30s already edited and published several anthologies of poetry and a biography of Sarah, Duchess of Marlborough. During our tenancy of the flat she went on to produce *Beau Brummell: a*

Kathleen Gettins

Biographical Study and worked on a life of George Eliot. She wrote under her first married name, Campbell.

7

She too had suffered a tragedy. Her daughter, Rosalind, had died of meningitis at the age of thirteen or fourteen. It was no secret that she looked upon me as something of a substitute. She often spoke of Rosalind. Rosalind and her elder brother, Denis, who was now an engineer lecturing at Oxford, were the children of Auntie Kathleen's first marriage. Our main living room, the Long Room, had once been their playroom. Our little plot of the garden had been their plot. Sandy, the marmalade cat which Jan and I petted, had been Rosalind's cat and various rhymes, games and Lear-like limericks invented by and for the Campbell children were now passed on to us.

The world's view of Kathleen Gettins would not have been an entirely gentle one, however. Her tongue was as sharp as her brain. Forthright, impatient, practising a form of humour best described as keen wit, she made no bones about her likes and dislikes. She adored cats, Italy, the Renaissance and nineteenth-century novelists, admired Oscar Wilde and was as scathing as only an entrenched highbrow can be about the sciences and modern playwrights. I can remember her laughing in gleeful appreciation over the sort of cynicism expressed by W.C. Fields in the statement: 'Anyone who hates dogs and children can't be all bad'.

Her manner of running the household upstairs was exactly expressed, to my mind, by the brisk, firm footfall which we could hear from below as she went sweeping along the hall. Mrs Milton, the Irish housekeeper, would give a little roll of her eyes to anyone nearby after AK's slender figure had spun in and out of the kitchen to deliver instructions.

Yet the compassionate side of her nature was readily aroused. Jean, the maid, assistant to Mrs Milton, lived in the very top flat of the house with a chap called Arthur. She was a fat girl and no one had guessed at her pregnancy until at eight months and three weeks she sheepishly announced it. Maybe she had thought she would be turned out of the house and her job. Far from it. Auntie Kathleen reacted splendidly. She organised the medical arrangements for feckless Jean, bought nappies and baby clothes and went about it all with kindness and reassurance.

Is there a degree of arrogance sometimes, though, to this taking people in hand and perhaps then assuming possessive rights over them? Admittedly this happened in Mother's case. We three had been offered the flat at a friend's behest at the end of the War when the hunt for housing was a desperate business; AK was also a champion of my mother in her handicapped situation as a lone woman. There was an element, however, of demanding companionship on outings and so forth, for which Mother hadn't the energy. Brushing aside whatever tasks Mother was engaged in, AK would say, 'Let's go for a run down to the coast!' But dropping everything for a spontaneous jaunt was not Mother's idea of enjoyment.

I was never quite a daughter substitute and at times the relationship was a fiery one, but the bonds of affection between us were always strong. Kathleen Gettins is etched in my memory as one of the most influential personalities I have ever encountered and intellectually we were well tuned. Discussing books remained a major source of mutual delight, whether it were to drool over Arthur Rackham's illustrations to *A Midsummer Night's Dream* or to differ as to whether Adam Bede should have married Dinah Morris. I also grew to share her love of Italy and much of her taste in art, for it was with her help a few years later that I was able to spend some months in Florence.

* * * * *

Our part of the grand old house, which had been built in about 1870, was the semi-basement, a snug nest tucked down halfway underground with the tall upper storeys rising proudly above it, yet resting upon it. We had three main rooms there and a large hall. After one or two rearrangements in the four years we had been there, we had settled upon a fairly comfortable division of function between these rooms.

Of the medium-sized rooms, the back one was the kitchen, the front one the sitting room and Mother's bedroom. It was here that the ceiling had come down. Besides Mother's divan,

9

My rather messy pen and ink sketch from back garden of 7 Wolsey Road, 1951

it held our three-piece suite, a rather elegant glass-fronted bookcase and the television set.

The kitchen, while furnished to the very simplest standard, boasted one rather luxurious appliance: an Ascot gas water heater, provided for us by my father who at that time was working for the manufacturers. It produced either warm, hot or boiling water at the turn of a knob. We could make tea from it straight into the pot with no need for a kettle.

The T-shaped hall took chests of drawers, a wardrobe shared by the three of us and a dressing table with a mirror. The largest room, the Long Room or Playroom, which echoed the dimensions of the drawing room above it, held divan beds for Jan and me and a huge built-in dresser full of our toys and books. It was our general playing and activity room, our painting and homework room. It was also the dining room,

10

The same view of the house, now used as business premises, in 1994.
Windows of our former kitchen here. [with arrow indicating]

containing the table and chairs from my parents' original home. There were, in addition, various smaller tables and a little desk that was mine, a floor-to-ceiling built-in cupboard filled, like the dresser, with toys, books and papers, and a great mantelpiece (but with its fireplace boarded up – we used an oil stove). Beneath one window stood a tank of tropical fish, a Christmas gift from my father in 1948.

Finally, to crown the contents of this splendid area, at the far end in the interior of the room stood the grand piano, a Blüchner I think. This was another relic of former times (for my father was a fine pianist), retained for the musical education of Jan and myself which unfortunately we failed to appreciate. The uphill work of getting me to practise had worn away Mother's wish for her daughters to have lifelong musical pleasure and fluency at their fingertips and by 1950 piano lessons had ceased.

11

I still tinkled the keys from time to time when I felt like composing a tune or when I was inspired by Christmas carols.

The basement also contained the boiler room and coal cellars. The former was at the back of the Long Room and here in its lair dwelt the monster boiler, a great black iron structure with a huge water cylinder above it and pipes like tree trunks designed to carry heat to the topmost attic of the house and to warm the high Victorian grandeur of its main upper floors. Alas, in those wintry post-war years it was more a case of tepifying than heating the place. The Colonel used to come down to stoke the boiler and dole it a few shovelfuls of coke, way below its appetite. But we in our flat had the best of it. It did not matter to us so much that the radiators were tepid. We had our oil stove and a coal fire in the sitting room, and even without these there was the fire in the belly of the old black monster itself which warmed our flat and which in winter could never be allowed to go out entirely. You could hang clothes round it to dry, as well, although they would tend to become sooty. Maybe the thing to remember most fondly about the boiler was its deliciously incongruous name, embossed in the iron of its side: The White Rose.

The cellars were not cellars in the sense of being at a still lower level than the rest of the basement. They were actually two small rooms opening from our hall, like walk-in cupboards or larders. One was used for storing coke but the other was never opened. It was the undisturbed darkness of this second one, I came to believe, that was the main nurturing ground in the house for a sinister form of life: huge spiders which emerged from time to time to terrify us.

* * * * *

It will be seen that the above tour of the flat has revealed no bathroom or lavatory, a deficiency Mother could never get used to, even though by now it was a long while since we had lived anywhere completely self-contained. Such practical difficulties of the place naturally weighed more upon her than they did on Jan and me, so that while we girls could love the flat without reservation, the driving impulse of her life in those years was to attain a better home.

Meanwhile, our facilities were upstairs. There was a flight of stairs from our hall with a door at the top which opened into the Gettins' hall, close to the back door and the kitchen. Our lavatory, with its truly nineteenth-century mahogany bench seat across the width of the little room, was opposite the door of the kitchen. Fortunately, one feat of endurance that was not demanded of us in those harder times was to go creeping up to such a place in the middle of the night. Like almost everyone else, we kept chamber pots under our beds. It wasn't only having your privy down the garden or needing to light a candle to go through a dark house that kept this venerable custom going. My grandparents, in a house dating from only just before the war, still had their pot or 'po' under the bed, for it could be bitterly cold to venture more than a couple of yards beyond your eiderdown.

Although the bench-seated lavatory was more or less designated to be for our use, the bathroom had to be shared and to reach it we were obliged to advance to the front part of the main hall and take another flight of stairs, laid with red carpet, to a sort of mezzanine floor from which nothing opened other than the bathroom. It was this journey that to my mother was more disagreeable than any other aspect of not having a bath to ourselves. Generally going up there at a time when nobody else would require the room, she felt embarrassed to be seen, carrying her towel and toilet things, as she passed the doors of the dining room and drawing room, where the Gettins might have guests. And then afterwards she would either have the nuisance of getting fully dressed again or would have to go down in a dressing gown past those doorways once more.

The bathroom itself was a fine-looking place, spacious and tiled in white and green marble over every inch of floor and walls. The Colonel's leather razor strop hung from the radiator. However, the hot water came from a fearsome and fairly dangerous gas geyser, giant older brother to our Ascot.

In 1950, I believe, Jan and I were still bathing together, for economy's sake and also because the whole business was such a performance. It was not thought safe for us to light the geyser ourselves. Two baths a week were about enough, and on other nights we washed at the kitchen sink. 'Face, neck and ears!' were Mummy's nightly instructions, issuing as one word: 'Faceneckandears', but there are hints in the Diary that she did not trust us to do the job properly ourselves, because once or twice when she was out or busy I noted that I 'washed myself' as though it were an exception.

There was one other amenity for which we had to go up to the main part of the house, and that was the telephone. It stood on a small table in the hall, not far from the doorway of our flat. I don't know what arrangements were made between Mother and the Gettins to pay for our share of the calls but we seemed to have fairly free use of it. The phone number was 'Molesey Nine Double One'.

* * * * *

We three with Auntie Kathleen on Hampton Court Bridge circa 1948

14

Tuesday January 3   Went to Kingston. Bought two books with my tallies. Watched Custer's Last Stand *on TV.*
Had hair washed. After tea read new books, 'Poisonous Fungi' and 'Edible Fungi'

Hair washing was a fortnightly ritual sufficiently time consuming to merit a mention in the Diary almost every time it happened through the year. A two week interlude between washes, prolonged on some occasions by illness, might now seem to betray very grubby habits, yet Mother was decidedly fastidious. The geyser and the rinsing with numerous jugs of water (no spray) would not have deterred her if she had believed it necessary to wash our hair more frequently, but our ways reflected the usual standards of the time. Before the existence of conditioners and, even more important, before the beehive hairdo and the wilder styles of later decades, there was nothing desirable in the fly-away fluffiness of freshly washed hair. 'I can't do a thing with it!' was indeed the trite but heart-felt cry of the clean headed. The ideal was smooth hair and, even if curly, the hair had to be seen to be under control. We'd have given guineas for some lacquer. Tendrils over the ears and escaping stray strands were the bane of their bearers. The cultivated tangles of today, had some young 1980s, or '90s, woman appeared among us then, would have been incomprehensible. Hair only achieved its prime condition five to seven days after washing.

Drying was a slow process. As my hair had not been cut since I was about five, it was very long and I don't think we had a dryer. Sometimes I would kneel on the floor bending my head down in front of an electric fan heater, hair spread in all directions, probably quite a dangerous practice, but mostly my crowning glory was left to dry in its own good time.

And why, you may ask, were these burdensome tresses, which also required to be plaited each morning, not cropped in a more practical fashion? Partly out of Mother's pride, I admit, but also to avoid jumping from the frying pan into the fire. If it had not been for the plaits every morning it would have meant curlers every night. For, excluding the girl with a very short bob (with a bow in it), one simply could not go around with *straight* hair, goodness no!

* * * * *

The front entrance to the flat, opening into our hall, was approached from the outside by descending a flight of seven deep stone steps. It was at the same side of the house as the stable wing. This consisted of what was now the garage, immediately abutting the main part of the building, with space enough to have once accommodated a couple of carriages, and then extending beyond this, rustled over by the lime trees above its slate roof, stood stabling for a pair of horses, with their stalls and mangers, an anvil and shelving for all the

Number 7 Wolsey Road, now Cardinal House. The stable block on left converted into offices. Our front door formerly in the angle between main house and stables.

accoutrements still intact. Since it had a doorway at both back and front, we children could chase through the stable and round the whole house.

From the street you could hardly see our stairwell for shrubs and trees. Masses of red and white hawthorn blossom glorified that corner in the spring. Images return of clattering down those seven steps with Paul and the Fermor girls on a hot day into the shadiness below. We were blithe in our disregard of the struggle against dirt and dampness in the flat. Those were adult worries. Jan and I were simply rooted in the place as deeply and naturally as if we were the trees, and our shared memory of having had a rich and happy childhood springs largely from the nine years spent in Wolsey Road.

* * * * *

The school term for Jan and me did not begin until January 11th. Some extracts show how we filled the winter days.

Wednesday January 4   Smithy came to mend ceiling in morning and afternoon.

We played after lunch then went to palace. Quite a lot of people there. Fed ducks at long water and stream. Walked home through Wilderness as dusk was falling. Mummy came home from first day back at college at about 4. p.m.

Thursday January 5   Smith came again to do ceiling. Seems to have got no further than before. Played. Made it up with Paul and Pat. Saw TV at Paul's. Custer's Last Stand, an orchestra playing, film of Australia.

Mummy not home till 7.30.

Friday January 6   Jan and I went for walk in the palace. Fed the ducks. Not so many people out as on Wednesday. Weather is colder but fresh. Went to Dutch Garden.

Susan Braybrook's party in evening, 6.0 p.m. Had a buffet supper, smashing games. Nice boy called Gordon there. Came home 9.30.p.m.

Monday January 9   A.M. Went to palace about 11.0. Fed ducks as usual. Only about two other people there. Little robin

17

came and sat next to us, and a chaffinch perched a few inches away from my shoulder! Had a drink on the way home at approx. 12.30.

P.M. Painted pictures for Latin book. Played after tea in the garden, though dark. Mummy home about 6.15.

In all during that holiday, two parties and a pantomime imparted a swell of seasonal excitement to the smooth currents of our regular routines which consisted of shopping, watching television, playing with our friends, painting, reading and helping with household tasks. The first of the special occasions, Susan Braybrook's party on January 6th, was evidently arranged to be a rather sophisticated occasion for a girl reaching her teens, its late hours serving to distinguish it from the parties of *little* girls. I am sorry to say, however, that the suggestion of any interest in boys on my part is a solitary reference and that nice Gordon will not be heard of again in the Diary.

Our principle activities, in terms of hours devoted to them, appear to have been watching the TV and walking in the Palace, providing an excellent balance for the time of year between indoor and outdoor pursuits.

Hampton Court Palace, loved and familiar to us, was like the great house at the heart of an estate to which we belonged. We had a great sense of ease and freedom in going around. Molesey's position on a pleasantly flat and accessible sort of terrain, along with the fact that Jan and I had the use of several extensive gardens (none of them belonging to us) close by, made it seem that the whole district was open to us. In 1946 it had symbolised our feelings of having found a haven at last by coming to live in this beautiful area where the Palace grounds, the parks, the Green and the river all lay within walking distance. No wonder 'Peacetime' had meant not only the end of the War but a settling down and the hope of finding our personal peace.

Our walk to the Palace took barely ten minutes: along Bridge Road, where we were known to almost every shopkeeper, and over the fine balustraded span of the bridge

18

that arches across the Thames. From the moment of reaching the southern side of the river we were able to view our objective on the other bank and to see how it is turned perpetually as if to look for the arrival of the Court from London at the landing stage. Sometimes Jan and I would descend to the towpath and follow this approach but generally we entered by the main gateway, simply walking up the drive, into the Base Court and on through the gardens with all the presumption of a couple of courtiers. Perhaps one reason for our feeling so at home there was that Jan had gone to school in the Palace for a couple of years, as one of about 30 infants in a single class, like a village school, with two teachers in a couple of rooms which are now probably offices.

One of the prime qualities of Hampton Court is the openness of its aspect, which is like that of few other grand buildings. Not at any point in approaching it do you climb even one step. It is almost all on the level, with just the gentlest of slopes leading towards the entrance. Before we moved to Molesey, the word Palace had conjured up in my mind an image of shining, conical towers rising loftily from a marble edifice, but when Auntie Kathleen took us to see it for the first time I found there was nothing lofty or shining about the real Palace. There it stood in all its Tudor tranquillity, its moat a grassy trough, its drawbridge a gravel driveway. Rather than marble towers it boasted a forest of fantastically wrought chimneys. In some way, however, it combined homeliness with grandeur. Not for a moment was I disappointed in it. Its strong warm brick has something about it of its most notable occupant, Henry, at his best, ruddy and sturdy and standing as Holbein saw him, squarely on both feet. Mother was a tremendous admirer of the Tudors.

The 400 years since gangs of bricklayers had swarmed about the site creating the structure to the Cardinal's command had given the Palace an air of gravity and domestic repose. Princes had stormed and stamped their tantrums in its galleries, had danced their revelries among spilled flagons under the smoking torchlight, and had departed from it. The War had not scarred it but had left it sombre and still listening, one felt, to be certain the gunfire had finished. This was a quiet period for the Palace and in my mind the winter coolness and bare flower beds of those January walks only enhanced the sense of a very personal and local attachment. Sometimes we would walk right through to Home Park. Even if one of us were on her own, we scarcely worried about safety, other than being careful not to go too close to the deer in the autumn.

* * * * *

For the winter months at least, it must be admitted that watching television outstripped walking as a major leisure pastime of Jan and myself, for there sat the TV, in term time and holidays alike, and available on any day of the week when, after school, it would have been too dark to go out.

Remarkably enough, we had possessed a TV set since before the War. My father had been working at HMV in Hayes and he was able to acquire, sometimes for home testing, many appliances and luxury items not generally found on the average semi-detached housing estate in the 1930s.

After our parents separated, there came a period of unsettled, stopgap moves in and out of furnished places, or of being with Nanny and Gagga, and the TV set went into storage with our other furniture.

Triumphantly, it was restored and tuned in, at 7 Wolsey Road, in time for the first major post-war broadcast, the Victory Parade in June 1946. We packed a crowd of relatives and friends into our sitting room that day to gaze at the little grey screen across which the troops marched past in a drizzly rain while the King took the salute – or rather, we gazed at a reflection of the screen. The long cathode ray tube pointed upwards, encased in a polished cabinet that stood as high as a sideboard and the picture showed in a mirror on the inner surface of the lid.

Although in 1950 television broadcasting was still scheduled for only a limited time each day, Mummy made us choose a selection of programmes for the week rather than indulge in indiscriminate viewing. Despite this, I must have been an addict.

20

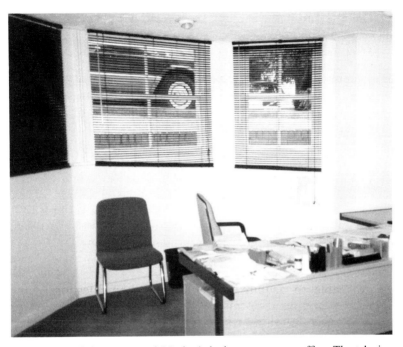

Our former sitting room and Mother's bedroom, now an office. The television stood under the middle window.

Sunday January 8 In afternoon watched TV but sound had gone. Was funny watching and hearing nothing.
Sunday January 15 Watched TV although no sound.

Evidently the week of waiting for repair was too much for me. I was prepared to sit in front of a silent screen. And on one more evening later in the year I admitted a serious lack of self restraint: *Tons of prep. I shouldn't have watched TV on and off from 5.0 till 6.15 p.m. I did, however, and was working till 8.0 p.m.*

This shows that maybe the rules were not so strict, especially when Mummy came home late. Jan and I also took any chance to watch in the houses of friends, for we soon ceased to be unique in our ownership of a TV.

The programmes we saw through the year, beginning with the circus at 'Olimpia' on 1st January, included *Custer's Last Stand*, *Let's Make an Opera*, *Fire over England*, newsreels and numerous other films, plays and concerts. *Muffin the Mule* was still going strong while memorable series of the future were starting up – *Men of Action*, for instance, on November 16th. I am somewhat puzzled by the Diary entry of 14th June that *They have a special children's programme on Wednesday now from 5 to 6 p.m.* as there obviously had always been broadcasts for children. Only once do I seem to have been critical of a programme, when it was *Women's Hour or something uninteresting*.

Jan and I were dedicated to Westerns, particularly our regular favourite *The Range Busters* which featured a trio of cowboys named Dusty, Crash and Alibi. Four years earlier, it had been a cowboy film which inspired the creation of the Gang. Adventure stories of any kind tended to result in a rush to the garden the moment they were over to begin acting out our own version of the drama. During the Easter holidays, while we were staying with Uncle Ken and Auntie Barbara in Guildford, a serial called *Mystery Squadron* seems to have been shown every day for about a week. I think it was to do with fighter planes. If it was not raining too hard for us to go out, *Mystery Squadron* would then be replayed by us on each subsequent day's trip to Grassy Hill, as we called the nearest segment of the Hogsback.

We loved the radio almost as much as TV. All three of us, Mummy, Jan and I, and often no doubt our 'help', Mrs Shubert (of whom more anon), would listen if we could to those favourite old comedies, *Up the Pole*, *Ignorance is Bliss* and *Take it from Here*.

By 1950 nearly everyone we knew had a television set and we exploited our friends without scruple. One morning in July, Jan quarrelled with Paul and *came home sobbing*. However, *Paul came over in evening. He was very sorry, kissed Jan, all's well. Good thing, as we wanted to watch his T.V. because a fly got in our set and it's not working now*. Phew! Disaster averted!

* * * * *

On January 4th, while Jan and I were feeding ducks, for Mummy the Christmas holiday was over. It was the beginning of the second term at the Hampton Teacher Training College. Those were the days of the Emergency Training Scheme which was designed to restock the teaching profession after its thin times in the War, also to reduce the size of classes and to prepare for the post-war baby boom. The latter generation of babies must have been on the threshold of school life in 1950 but not for several years would any of them find themselves in a classroom as Mrs Appleby's pupils, for it was the secondary school age that she would be teaching.

When she applied to train, she had been urged to take an advanced course that would have led to a grammar school post and specialisation, in economics perhaps. The selection committee must have been rather impressed by her abilities. In 1933 Mother had won a State Scholarship, a far more rare attainment before the War than it later became, and had entered into a life no person in all her family had ever known, university life, at the London School of Economics. In the third year there, her marriage and my arrival had put an end (rather tragically, I always thought) to her studies before she could graduate, but the State Scholarship and university experience, even without a degree, stamped their hallmark clearly enough. The training colleges, in their thirst, were taking people with no academic qualifications at all, not even Matric.

Tempting as it was, however, Mother turned down the option of the grammar school course. It would have entailed journeying to a college much farther from home than Hampton and she could see that in view of the intensive work of the 13 months that lay ahead, it would be wise to make all the practical conditions of her life as simple as possible. Besides, on a point of principle she felt that the best qualified people should not be automatically channelled into the grammar schools; the secondary moderns should have their share.

One of the other practical conditions for which she had to

23

make plans was finding somebody to look after Jan and me, and thus Shoo came into our lives.

One day, before training started in the summer of 1949, Mother placed a postcard in a newsagent's window advertising for a mother's help. A woman who usually bought her cigarettes at a different newsagent's felt prompted that morning for some reason to go instead to the one Mother had just been into. 'The ink was barely dry,' the legend goes. The shopkeeper was only at that very minute pinning the card to his board when along came Mrs Shubert. She read it and immediately walked round to Wolsey Road. After a short conversation, Mother saw no need to interview anyone else nor to take time making a decision and she employed Mrs Shubert on the spot.

On Mother's first day at college, Jan and I arrived home eager to meet the strange lady who would give us our tea and stay with us every evening until Mummy returned. There she sat, upright on a kitchen chair, with hands folded in her lap. Her face was lined but, just as Mummy had said, there was a bright dab of rouge on each cheek and her mouth was slightly crookedly reddened. Wispy pale hair fading from ginger to grey was gathered into a rather ramshackle chignon at the back of her head. Although she was not by any means fat, we saw that when she started moving around, preparing our tea, she walked with a slight waddle. Thick stockings covered varicosed calves.

She greeted us in a very direct, open manner, face to face as I remember (perhaps that was why she was seated, to be on a level with us), in a way which seemed to demand a reciprocal response. Consequently, we were not in the least shy with her.

She asked us keen, detailed questions about our school work and our favourite subjects. Shoo proved to be an educated, well-spoken, knowledgeable woman and as we came to know her we realised she must have once enjoyed a more comfortable background than her present lowly circumstances. Just how far she had come down in the world and what her social position had once been we were to discover eventually in Coronation Year, but what ill fortune it was that had brought her down we never found out. Her home was now a rented bedroom in the house of an Irish family in West Molesey. They were kind people, but Shoo was glad, one might even say desperately grateful, for the chance to fill her time usefully and responsibly.

She was supposed to come to us for only a couple of hours or so a day, to be there when Jan and I got home, to give us a meal, to wash up and perhaps do the ironing and to lay out some supper for Mummy. Soon she began arriving earlier and earlier and staying later and later. She cleaned the flat and did the washing, swept the ashes and lit the fire. Often when Mummy stayed late at college, Shoo saw us into bed and made sure our clothes were ready for the morning. She wanted no extra money and must have known there would be none, but simply adopted us as her family.

For the first few weeks, Auntie Kathleen kept an eye discreetly upon us while Mummy was out, but could only confirm Shoo's reliability and competence. In fact, she soon found she had much in common with her, for they had both, like the Colonel, lived in India for many years. Auntie Kathleen was able to verify Shoo's stories of life in the days of the Raj as authentic and this influenced everyone later on over what might otherwise have been treated as a most improbable claim, namely that Mrs Shubert was in fact Lady Suzanne Mary Marshall Shubert and in a different set of circumstances she would have been seated in Westminster Abbey in June 1953 for the crowning of the Queen. Divorce had apparently severed her from that exalted level of society and I am sure that, on the day she and Mummy first met, even without the rest of the story being revealed to begin with, the mere fact of a broken marriage was what kindled an instant flare of sympathy between the two of them.

Her eccentricities, her clairvoyance, her weaknesses and her sorrows were all facets of Shoo that came to light piecemeal over a period of time. But already by the beginning of 1950 her presence was so taken for granted that it was scarcely necessary to state in the Diary that when Mummy was not at home with us, Shoo almost always was.

* * * * *

Tuesday January 10   Packed satchel, etc., ready for school. In afternoon went to Pamela's ... Watched TV with her and played around. Went to panto in evening. Dick Whittington. Very good show. Not in bed till 11.p.m. Slept with Pamela.

Pamela was my 'best friend' and makes frequent appearances in the Diary, but the main comment to make about this occasion is that I find it astonishing that we were allowed to be up so late the night before term began. Earnest consultations would have taken place, I imagine, between Mummy and Mrs Fish, deploring the dearth of pantomime seats on more suitable evenings, and reasoning that it would be for 'just this once'.

It also means that I trundled over to New Malden with my school uniform and the packed satchel, so that Pamela and I would set off early the next morning together to begin the new term.

Pamela and myself in 1949

2

SWOTTING AND SWEATING

Wednesday January 11   A.M. Back to school, and am rather glad to be there. It's good to see everyone again and they're none the worse for the hols (I don't know what I thought might have happened to them.) *I am form captain and Sonja is vice. It's the third time I've been it.*

P.M. Needlework. Hols. have put Patty in good mood.

Mummy went to Rectory Farm school. She's on school prac. there. Mummy out in evening. Jan is vice form-captain in her form.

Unfortunately, I loved my school. Writers who as children suffered torments of bullying and injustice, who were abandoned in cold boarding schools by unfeeling parents and tyrannised by brutish masters, make far better biography than contented conformists. Not that I was a thorough conformist – but I was contented. School life suited me, particularly here at the Lady Eleanor Holles where by now the stability of remaining until my school days ended was assured. Having experienced six changes of schooling before the age of ten, with months of attendance missed altogether, owing to wartime upheavals, this was important.

The Lady Eleanor Holles School boasts a venerable foundation. It began as a charity school in the City of London in 1711, set up with money that the Lady Eleanor had left in her will for charitable purposes. By the last part of the nineteenth century it had started to expand and flourish with a vengeance. A great surge of energy was driving education forward then and it was especially a time for girls' schools to make leaps and bounds, the era of Miss Beale and Miss Buss. Many of them leapt and landed confidently on the high ground side by side with the boys' public schools.

The original tiny site for a couple of dozen poor children in Cripplegate had long been superseded by a mansion in Hackney, but by the 1930s the school had outgrown this too and another move was made. It was always impressed upon us, its latter day pupils, that ancient and modern had combined to our good fortune: we were blessed with a long history yet dwelt in a new building. The Duchess of Gloucester had officially opened the school in Hampton in 1937. There in wide playing fields, with the River Longford winding through the grounds, stood our handsome E-shaped centre of learning containing the latest and best of labs and library, gymnasium and lecture room, kitchens, classrooms and assembly hall.

On the far side of the fields from the main school was Burlington House, a nineteenth-century former residence which housed the junior department and where a small number of boarders could live, girls whose parents were overseas.

Jan was at present in Burlington House, in the form in which I too had started, the Lower Second, and would follow the same path in due course. She would 'take the scholarship', as we used to call sitting the Eleven Plus, and gain her free place in the senior school, our father having paid the fees of ten guineas per term while we were juniors.

* * * * *

Nearly six hundred girls from six to eighteen years old went streaming through the school gates that morning, a great chattering flock of grey coats brightened with the scarlet of hat bands, berets and ties.

Within the building the flock divided into lesser groups, each to its own familiar room and each child to her own desk, for this was not the Autumn Term, there would be no changes. Thirty or thirty-two of us, form Lower IV Y, congregated in Miss Tame's room on the first floor.

Miss Tame was a tall slim woman with rather a boney frame, as I remember; a teacher of mathematics. She taught the subdivision to which I belonged for this subject and her mild voice diminished somewhat the trepidation with which, for some strange reason, I had always approached the third R. I believe it was during this year with her that we were introduced to geometry and trigonometry, which I soon found the most congenial of the mathematical disciplines. We had already begun algebra.

The election of the Form Captain, alternatively known as Form Monitress, was the first thing that happened in each class on the first day of term. A form Games Captain was also chosen, but I think other posts, such as the blackboard monitress and people to look after books or flowers, were filled by volunteers. No girl could be Form Captain more than once in an academic year but, apart from the previous term's ineligible Captain and Vice-Captain, anybody could be nominated. It was purely a matter for the girls themselves and the only part played by the form mistress was to write the five or six nominations on the blackboard and help count the votes, which were by show of hands while the nominees waited outside the room. Scholastic achievement and other adult criteria did not enter into it because the person elected was meant to be someone the others would obey. This was the theory. *Miss Tame's afternoon off,* says the Diary one January day, and somewhat optimistically: *She told me before she went I was to make myself 'felt' and report anyone who misbehaved, etc.* I would have had no intention of following the second of these instructions but it shows that the Form Captain's job was one of the ways of teaching us to take responsibility.

I never heard of anyone actively seeking nomination for the post or canvassing for votes. As with other awards and attainments in any field of school life, etiquette demanded reticence and a show of astonishment, however mild, in a case of success. Self assertiveness in the form of: 'I think I'll do well' or 'I'm quite good at such and such' or 'I knew I'd win' would have been deplored as boastful. One bore one's own triumphs with muted pleasure.

Some might say I had nothing to boast about anyway regarding my responsibilities as Form Captain, for I failed to keep class behaviour up to scratch. In that year of the Lower IV our form was always in trouble. A sort of mass adolescent restlessness apparently took hold of us and afflicted especially a small number of girls among us who seemed unable to be good. This little group was always in the limelight and once they were in it they were caught out in every minor misdemeanour. In mitigation, it must be said that they might have been victims of circumstance. The staff, I am certain, would have been very much on their toes at the time and their scrutiny particularly sharp, for that January marked only the third month in office of a new headmistress, who was like an eagle over the school.

The main miscreants were some of the brightest girls in the class, good at work and games, and popular. The crimes they committed were things like making a noise, behaving badly in buses on the way home, not wearing hats in the street, being out of bounds or coming into the school by a prohibited entrance and excessive talking in class. Probably there was a spirit of general rowdiness, of being cheeky to prefects and of producing poor quality work. The most serious offences would be those which expressed direct disobedience or insolence, or which broke school rules.

There was one unlucky member of staff who was utterly unable to keep order, in whose lessons the behaviour of the entire class was decidedly dreadful. Although we rarely acted so deliberately with malice, I daresay poor Miss Tame and all our teachers found us hard to deal with.

We were, however, reckoned to be, and were conscious ourselves of being, a particularly strongly united and likeable form. The badness, by the way, applied strictly to Lower IV Y, not to our sister form, the Xs; they were different from us and larger numbers of them gained high marks in exams, but they did not have our great solidarity. There was some kind of passion in us which they lacked. Mother in her teaching years would agree that every class of children has its own character. Ours was full of a turbulent, mettlesome and maybe bewildered spirit, which for a few months possessed us.

* * * * *

Thursday January 12 Had English with new mistress. Name: Miss Bishop (Bish). Fairly nice.

It's been very foggy. We were let out at 3.5 p.m. All the same we had to walk. No buses. Four of us went together. All got buses or walked in the end but Pam. Rang her mother and stayed night with me. Smashing fun. She slept in small camp bed which I did not know Mummy had, in a pair of my pyjamas.

Friday January 13 Fog cleared. Went to school with Pam, who had breakfast here. Everyone got home safely apparently last night.

Juniors came over to prayers with us. I received monitress badge in P.T.

Miss Tame away in afternoon.

Mummy home early. Shoo went out to pictures. Cosy evening: painted and read.

I remember that foggy day so well. Although the word 'smog' is not used in the Diary, this is what it most certainly was – one of the notorious London smogs. Through the school windows we saw it thickening with that distinctive yellow soupiness that seemed more dense than ordinary fogs.

The walk home was full of gaiety and eeriness, and for me only about three miles long, following the usual trolleybus route along Hampton High Street to where, by Hampton Church, it meets the road to Hampton Court running between the river and the tall iron railings of Bushy Park.

The others had further to go but the most distant of all from her home was Pamela. She depended upon three buses to take her stage by stage to New Malden. When she was first sent to LEH her family had been living in Wraysbury, near Windsor, and as a little nine-year-old she had plied back and forth on a complicated daily itinerary of both buses and trains, taking heaven knows how long. From New Malden it was not that much better. Our normal pattern was to meet each other in the mornings at Hampton Court Green from where we picked up the 667 trolleybus, but whereas I had just walked over the bridge, Pamela had at this point already left home an hour

31

before. She was not the only girl to come so far to school but very few indeed were brought by car.

The solution for many was to cycle, but this choice would not have been open to me. On the night I was born, the doctor who delivered me had recently had to attend a case of a fatal accident to a child cyclist. He asked Mother to promise never to let me ride a bike and in the fervour of new motherhood she agreed.

Mother's vow might well have lapsed if I had badgered her over the matter, for without any quibble Jan was given a bicycle. But I was indifferent to it. Pamela tried once or twice to teach me, on her own bike, in the quiet roads of Malden. I was not adept. I had no faith whatever in being able to balance on those ridiculous narrow strips of rubber, despite seeing hundreds of other people do so, and when propelled forward along the pavement by a push from Pamela at the back of the saddle, I stiffened with panic rather than try to work out how it was done.

* * * * *

The new term had not run a full week before the illnesses began.

Sunday January 15 A.M. Have caught Jan's cold. Did not go out today. Started making a set of mosaics.

By Monday I had *got a shocking cold and sore throat and running eyes and toothache. Most people are in the same state.* On Tuesday: *Pamela absent. She had a sore throat yesterday. Perhaps it's worse. My cold is not much better.* And by Wednesday: *Pamela back much better. My cold much worse. Cannot play games so had fun watching Upper IV B doing gym with Julia Gaffyne ... Feeling rotten by bed time.*

Finally on Thursday I had to stay at home. *Away from school today. Did not want to stay home in the least, for it would be Art at school. Sonja will be glorifying over me tomorrow cause she'll have taken my place as form captain.*

Made some more mosaics, painted, read half of 'Good Wives' and wrote some poems. I do feel much better for this day in bed.

32

Friday January 20 Horrors! Still at home! Missing Gym, History, English. Pamela rang me up this evening. She said I did not miss much in the French and Latin lessons. Apparently Sonja is in raptures. I don't feel so good as last night.

Note the power struggle implicit in those remarks about poor Sonja. This is not a passage in the Diary that I am proud of. I seem to have been a jealous little leader and the declaration of horror over being kept at home now sounds decidedly priggish.

The 'shocking cold' was only the first of many illnesses that year. Seven times in all I had to miss school for a few days. Early in March the pattern was repeated of Pamela's being absent with a sore throat and my going down like a domino the next day. And so it went on. Auntie Kathleen used to say '*Another* cold?' regarding me as rather a weakling in this respect. Certainly I was not robust but the Diary shows Jan and Pamela and many of our classmates to have been equally susceptible. We caught colds or flu or what would probably now be called 'a virus'; we were sick and had stomach aches or simply 'felt pretty bad'.

Although quite clearly we were passing infections around to one another, I feel our resistance was lowered by another factor: we were never warm enough. Setting off for school on a winter's morning we would be clad in seemingly snug clothing. We would have jumpers or cardigans over our blouses, with grey skirts and grey woollen overcoats. Scarves, hats, knee-length grey socks with stout black lace-up shoes – all these items presented an apparently well-fortified front to the weather and at the innermost layer would be the redoubtable liberty bodice (still just about tolerable to a girl until her chest started to fill out), quite possibly with a Chilprufe vest as well and quite positively with the school uniform lock-knit grey knickers.

Yet all this lacked one vital ingredient – draught-proofing. A huge amount of body heat must have been lost at the Great Knee Gap, where your skin got chapped and purple. The sleeves of the coat had no storm cuffs or welts and the hat or beret could not cover your ears. Tights and anoraks would have saved me much pain.

The worst thing was to be cold and wet. You faced a dilemma, for if instead of the overcoat you wore a gabardine raincoat and instead of outdoor shoes, Wellington boots, the cold would penetrate more easily. In any case, these garments gave only partial protection against rain and snow because schoolchildren did not carry umbrellas.

We arrived at school, therefore, after a walk from the bus (slightly less than a mile) sometimes very damp indeed, our hands frozen in sodden woollen gloves. All the outer garments were hung in the cloakrooms where they had little chance of drying to any perceptible degree before you went out in them again. The cloakrooms, close to the entrance where doors swung to and fro ceaselessly as pupils arrived, were in the most exposed and far-flung limb of the building. At least, however, you could change there into indoor shoes, which were kept in the shoebag on your peg.

The next half an hour should have helped to warm the blood. There would be the brisk business of getting to your form room, hurrying to be on time; milling round unpacking your satchel, then answering the register, then trooping down to the hall for Prayers, standing in a body of about 350 people and filling your lungs with hymn singing.

But then came the hours of sitting at lessons in rooms whose wide expanses of windowpane had been designed in a vision of bright young minds bathed in sunlight and airiness, yet which in winter were merely great glass screens letting the coldness in. The heating seemed to me to be always just below what was needed. I remember days on end of chilliness and of the member of staff who stood before us leaning against the nearest radiator as often as she could.

Twice a day, at mid-morning and after lunch, we were sent out for 'break' or recess and came in again with frozen fingers and feet, only to sit once more in a tepid classroom. After every games lesson the hearty girls cooled down and the inactive ones, like me, huddled in the same indifferent temperature. Every visit to the lavatory meant going out to the farthest arm of the cloakroom block and enjoying another bracing blast through the swing doors.

It was all taken to be absolutely normal. I recall it now but at the time I am sure there was only a background awareness of it and I daresay our brains were kept alert by the coolness. As for our bodies, though, I think it very likely that half our ailments were not proper colds but chills. We were suffering from exposure.

* * * * *

Monday January 23 Back to school today at last. (I had missed only two days.) *Sonja is glad to have me back, after all! She's not been enjoying her responsibilities as much as she expected to.*

Dear Sonja, I hope to goodness I did not go back crowing over you, in contradiction of all I have said about the school code of self effacement. If I did, however, our rivalry was soon to be eclipsed by a power contest on a larger scale. The school was to have a Mock Election. I had returned just in time for the excitement of the first meeting. The 1950 general election was due and the occasion was to be used to teach the entire school something about politics. For some reason, perhaps to fit in with the exam timetable or something of that kind, our mock election took place a full month before the real thing. I don't quite know what happened at that first meeting. In all likelihood it was to explain the procedure to us, but anyhow the greater interest came with the speeches of the various candidates, which we listened to over subsequent days.

Tuesday January 24 Went to a Communist meeting in break. Jean Rogers is candidate. She made a good speech, showing up good Comm. points and leaving out bad ones, as they always do. We all applauded and booed at the right time.

Wednesday January 25 Went to a Conservative meeting in break. Colgate is candidate. Very good speaker. Much better than the Labour candidate, Austin, who spoke in lunch hour. She got more boos than the others, I think.

Thursday January 26 Went to Liberal meeting in break. Candidate, Maybrey, did not speak very well.

After school stayed to important meeting of all candidates. All got booed except Conservative. It's the poll tomorrow. Everyone very excited. Pity we're not allowed to vote.

Friday January 27 We missed Latin this afternoon to hear mock election results. Conservative 127 votes. Labour 28 votes. Liberal 21. Communist 4!

Loud cheers for all. Miss Denney was cheered and stamped because she arranged it all.

We came home at 3.5.p.m.

The total electorate of 180 suggests that voting was limited to the Lower Fifth and above. This would have demonstrated to us that eligibility came with maturity (relatively speaking) but whether one was eligible to vote or not, our mock election ensured that by the time the nation as a whole went to the polls we took a keen interest in the matter.

Thursday February 23 Election today. Up the Liberals!

Friday February 24 No-one has talked of anything but Election. Had school radio on at lunch. Most of us cheered at Tory victories. Radio was on all day at home. Programmes changed and intirupted. Tory won in our district, but they announced Labour as leaders [i.e., in the country as a whole]. *Jan and Mummy at home.*

Up the Liberals, eh? The interesting thing about this is that it means my mother must have been voting Liberal, because I myself at the age of thirteen would have had no conception of cheering for any party other than by her influence. Whether she actually managed to go to the polls and vote in that particular election I cannot tell, for she had been ill all the week and was in bed on the Monday and Tuesday, but the point is that support for the Liberal Party indicates a change in her allegiance. She had most definitely voted Labour in 1945 and the reason I am so sure of this is that I have a very sharp memory of a conversation that she and I had had at the time. With eight-year-old insouciance I had declared that this grown-up thing called an election was of no interest to me, and she had rounded on me quite vehemently. 'Oh yes it is!' she cried. 'It's to do with your future. It's very important!' So that was my first lesson in party politics, and Mother's own written records, as well as the testimony of other members of the family, have since borne out my impressions about where her loyalties lay both before and all during the War.

Mother sprang from a family with intense political views and her studies at school and university had centred around politics and economics. The Joneses were socialists and communists, even being active in party work in brief bursts, although mostly their participation took the form of fierce discussion round the meal table at home. At any rate, the subject exercised their minds, I would say, to a greater degree than average. The Jones household never observed the dictum that sex, religion and politics were matters banned from polite conversation.

But how did Mother come to that shift of opinion within a space of five years, from labour to liberal? There are several possible explanations. One factor might have been disenchantment with the Attlee government. One might have been the new intellectual contacts she had made in the years since moving to Wolsey Road and especially the views of Kathleen Gettins, who I know was a liberal, and who seems to have been locally active within the party because, on February 12th, says the Diary, Jan and I *helped Auntie Kathleen stamp letters for the Election.*

KG and her circle, I feel, personified a traditional admiration for all things moderate, for the middle road. This would have appealed to Mother. It was the way of the philanthropic thinking person, of the academic intelligentsia, and accorded well with the profession of teaching. The newspaper we read was *The News Chronicle*, a liberal paper which was also regarded as the 'teachers'' paper because it devoted so much space and emphasis to educational matters. Everything fitted in.

While these would have been quiet and private influences, though, a more urgent pressure began exerting itself: McCarthyism. In this country, McCarthyism was probably a more suppressed force than it was in the United States but, nevertheless, it produced some serious reds-under-the-beds reflexes. In many professional quarters, alarms were set clanging which perhaps turned out to be false warnings, but people ran for cover just the same. I have sometimes wondered how Mother was affected. It is impossible for me to be sure of the truth but I have one small significant piece of evidence to go on. At some time, not in 1950 but perhaps in 1951, I watched her throw her old textbooks of Lenin and Marxism on to a bonfire in the garden. I can remember smatterings of conversations, too, between her and Uncle Ken or Uncle John, about a teacher known to have lost her job and I know that there was felt to be true danger in possessing the traces of having once saluted, if not actually carried aloft, the people's flag of deepest red. Undoubtedly Mother would have feared for her own future career and, above all, for her children.

The greater part of the nation at the time, however, did not equate our mild and familiar British form of socialism with the cold war enemy and elected to continue being governed by Mr Attlee, for just a little longer at any rate.

* * * * *

Saturday January 28 Have saved 3/- towards Jan's birthday. Had a lot of shopping. Spent all afternoon doing a self-portrait. Not all that good. Read Mystery at Witchend after tea.

Mystery at Witchend! One of the literary landmarks of my life, a bright beacon of a book, but one that burned too late and without passing on its message to the next hilltop across the land. *Mystery at Witchend* by Malcolm Saville was indeed a mystery, the story of a crime solved by children. Hundreds of stories like it exist. It gripped me. I never read anything so avidly. The real mystery, though, is why did I not read with that kind of passion more often?

The answer is that I rarely read that type of book. From the very beginning, my reading matter had been carefully monitored. A taste for the classics was cultivated, and Gagga used to give me copies of Dickens and Kipling from the time I was seven or eight, while from my father I received adult text books on art and artists and natural history. The ones bought by Gagga were frequently second-hand editions chosen by him for their fine binding as well as the content. Undoubtedly he intended them to last my lifetime, which they have done, and the inscriptions inside their covers reveal the most lovingly expressed purpose of nurturing my taste and my mind.

Yet there is one regret: that I was made too self-conscious, too soon, of having to discriminate between 'good' and let us say 'popular' literature. Enid Blyton was barred, for example, not for any of the reasons that swept her away from the public libraries years later but because she used too limited a vocabulary or was too simple and unstimulating. For a few weeks at one stage Jenny Bellears lent me her copies of Enid Blyton's little magazine, *Sunny Stories*. Then Mummy took a look at it and decided it was not up to scratch. I had to tell Jenny not to bring me *Sunny Stories* any more and I can still feel the undercurrent of embarrassment that accompanied this, for I sensed the implied criticism of Jenny's own and her parents' literary standards. For a long while comics were banned too, except as holiday treats, although this rule had been relaxed by 1950.

Another children's writer who had come under a cloud of disapproval was A.A. Milne. I had a copy of *When We Were Very Young* that someone had given me in my infancy but as a whole the Winnie the Pooh stories found no favour in our household. The trouble lay in the decadent social background of Christopher Robin. The poor twee little boy had a nanny, something to be frowned upon by all respectable middle-class and working-class mothers, so I never became familiar with Kanga and Tigger and the other characters that people seem to love so much. On the other hand I knew the lovely magic wood of *The Tree that Sat Down* by Beverley Nichols, and its sequel, *The Stream that Stood Still*. For both these enchanting stories I have Auntie Kathleen to thank.

One occasion of immediate and definite censorship of my reading occurred in this year of 1950 when Uncle John very sensibly stopped me looking at one of his scientific journals that contained an illustrated clinical article about cancer. This, however, is something I remember independently of the Diary, for the Diary is regrettably uninformative about my reading matter for that year. I used to record the fact that I had spent time reading, but only a few of the books are named. They include only three items of fiction, *Good Wives*, *David Copper-field* and *Silas Marner*, of which the last two were part of the school syllabus.

The undesirable result, I think, of the strong emphasis on the quality of my books was a sense of inhibition and a failure to share with other children entry into some of the worlds that writers create. It might also have led to my being a physically slow reader. Could it be that by devouring anything that comes their way, from the age of nine or ten, children develop a facility for taking in everything more rapidly? Certainly I read a good deal; I was not put off reading, not by any means, but some of my books took a fair amount of chewing and digesting. And the precept was writ large and clear that pleasure alone was not sufficient reason for reading something.

As in the case of bicycle riding, things were far more relaxed when it came to Jan, which they so often are with younger siblings. The rot had set in, I suppose, from her very babyhood, when sudden dashes to and from the air raid shelter at all times of the day or night had caused the collapse of all the old rigid four-hourly feeding schedules which our parents had faithfully followed before the War. The Diary shows, for example, that Jan was allowed to take regular delivery of a comic, *The Dandy*, in 1950, while I was set in my ways by then and subscribed to the far more respectable *Children's Newspaper*. It is probably a mistake in a child who *has* under-gone the rigid feeding schedules not to make the effort to be a little more wilful and rebellious, but I did not learn this for a very long time.

But setting aside these minor criticisms of my upbringing, I must offer thanks, which Jan would join me in, for one of the bookly gifts placed before us both. It was not one book but ten, and the name associated with them was not an author but an editor – Arthur Mee, creator of *The Children's Encyclo-paedia* (and incidentally founding editor of *The Children's Newspaper* too). Having seen the set that had belonged to Denis and Rosalind in the 1930s, Mother bought us one by one as they came out the ten volumes of the new post-war edition, for when it came to books and educational extras she generally found the money somehow. On the face of it, she must have disapproved of some of the general ethos of the *Encyclopaedia* (for though we had moved over to the middle of the political spectrum we were still obstinate dissidents in many ways – anti-nationalistic, anti-monarchist, anti-Empire) but had she examined it thoroughly she would have found little to argue with and would, in any case, have valued it as an unrivalled source of knowledge.

The Children's Encyclopaedia was set out not in the ordinary alphabetical format but in 'Groups' of subjects under headings such as Animal Life, Earth and Its Neighbours, Literature, Countries, The Bible, and so on, rather like the subjects of a school syllabus. Each Group contained chapters, usually of no more than a dozen pages, amply illustrated, offering a rough sort of optimum of what the young might be expected to absorb or need to know of any particular topic.

Arthur Mee intended to provide for the widest possible age range, as for instance within each poetry chapter where a couple of pages are always included of Little Verses for Very Little People; while the older child in the meantime can look to the Group headed 'Ourselves' and study Trade Between Nations or The Distribution of Wealth, can look under 'Art' and find The Greek and Roman Builders, and under 'Literature', The Literatures of the East. There is plenty of purely factual information for all ages, anything from The Picture Story of a Pair of Boots to Seaside Flowers In Colour. But Mee was far less concerned with listing facts than with explaining things, and he was concerned with ideas.

Within the Group headed 'Wonder' he poses and answers miscellaneous questions that children might ask, for instance, How far can we see? Must all things end? What are the Rules of the Road? Has the Earth ever been Weighed? and What are Logarithms? He then explores far more abstract themes such as Patriotism, Imagination, Instinct, Liberalism, Immortality. And it is through this sort of topic that the great strength of Mee's work comes out, for he is passionately uninhibited about expressing his own philosophy and it gives coherence to the whole edifice.

How to sum up this philosophy in a few words? I doubt if Jan and I as children understood the more profound qualities of the *Encyclopaedia* and may not even have read the more sophisticated and thought-provoking sections. But I would say that, if anything, the unity of mankind was Mee's lodestar. He was a Christian and a fervent patriot of the British Empire precisely because he saw both these institutions as forces for good in this cause.

His ideals were put forth with especial power in this, the post-war edition of his *Encyclopaedia* because although there had clearly not been time enough, and indeed no necessity, to alter the bulk of the contents from the pre-war editions, he had been able to bring it up to date with a supplement outlining events between 1939 and 1945 ('Hitler's War' as it is named) and a history of Germany describing the Führer's rise to power. The vehemence of the wording deserves quotation:

> ... *the burning of the Reichstag had a tremendous effect ... Fury was now let loose upon the Communists and the Jews, and terrible scenes of cruelty and violence followed. In this great turmoil Hitler succeeded in making himself dictator ... Jews were outlawed and declared unworthy to be citizens of a German State; thousands of them fled and those who stayed were subject to beating, torture and all forms of bitter humiliation ... Children were to learn military discipline and to be told that fighting was the finest thing in the world.*

Hitler's crime against the Jews was the more terrible because of what they, of all peoples, had given to the world. There is one startling passage when you think for a moment that you are seeing an endorsement of genocide and the concentration camps: '... *for all the earth was to be blessed in the ruin of Israel, and their destruction was to be the salvation of the whole earth ...*' until you realise that what is meant is the Diaspora, spreading '*Israel's sublime conception*', namely monotheism, and ultimately paving the way for Christianity.

'*The use of force to secure uniformity*' and '*men not allowed the liberty to be honest in their inmost beliefs'* were fearful evils which the British Empire stood opposed to, and '*It* [the Empire] *is ours to guard for freedom, for happiness and for peace ... That is the duty in which the boys and girls of today will have to take their share when they grow up.*'

These then were some of the ideals which Arthur Mee wished to instil into his readers, and he had no doubts as to his book playing its part in this. He closes it with a page entitled Farewell to the Book of my Heart, addressing his readers as '*My Little Travellers'*, travellers, that is, *'in this journey through the realms of knowledge'*, which again I feel is worth quoting:

> '... *the spirit of a book grows into our lives and will not die ... It will go on in your life as long as you see with these eyes and feel with these hands; and when these eyes no longer see, and these hands no longer feel, all that this book has meant to you will go on working in the lives of those who remember you. And after them, for ages after them, whatever is good in this book will live. Shall we let its last word breathe the spirit that I like to feel is in it everywhere, the spirit of goodwill to all mankind and the faith that ... nothing ill can happen to those who put their trust in God?'*

* * * * *

Exam time was upon us. Even while cheering and booing the election candidates we had begun to revise, for the countdown – *'exams in two weeks'* – had begun on 27th January.

Some members of staff apparently had the notion that we should be tested on what we had learned without the haphazard and often short-lived benefits of last minute cramming. For example *Miss Cooke* I wrote, *is not letting us do much revision for Biology.* And the following day (February 2nd) *Hebby has sprung a surprise on us. Part of exam (Dictée) starts tomorrow!* Hebby was as good as her word and the French *dictée* was *not very pleasant.*

Other teachers, however, encouraged us to revise and we

43

spent whole lessons as well as most of our homework time swotting. I'm sure it did good, in that it reinforced what we had been taught and was part of the utter thoroughness that I remember as a marked quality of the LEH education.

Monday February 6 Last science lesson before exam. Revised everything we could. More revision for homework. No R.I. exam thank goodness. Working doubly hard in nearly all other subjects. Had to miss Maths which I wanted to do well in and had (of all stupid things!) a hymn practice. Finished revising French, Latin tonight. Painted for Mummy. Feel very tired.

Tuesday February 7 Last minute rush to revise everything we can. Latin exam this afternoon. Not very fair, as we had never had some words. Did not finish. Did not like it much. Mummy home late. Got ourselves to bed.

Wednesday February 8 Geometry first this morning. Nice paper. Did all questions. Don't like having three per day. One can only revise in odd ten minuteses instead of whole 3 periods between break and lunch. English, after break. Nice easy paper. Biology in afternoon. Not bad. Did not finish.

Dropped a towel in bath tonight.

Thursday February 9 Algebra first thing this morning. Not so bad as I had expected. Lovely History. Easy but I did not finish. It's funny to see everyone when they come back, and the differing expressions on their faces.

French nice, finished before time.

Revised hard. Have been dreading Geog more than any.

Friday February 10 Nice Arithmetic paper. Finished it all.

We were able to go out to play at break.

Science reasonable. Did not finish.

Indoor lunch hour.

Could have done with at least 20 minutes to finish the Geography, but it wasn't a bad paper.

Glad exams are over. No homework.

We relaxed for the weekend, for not only had the examinations ended but it was half term, with the luxury of a Monday at home. At LEH we were never given a whole week off for half term, only one or two days. Forgetting that our principle holidays were probably long enough to compensate, I felt dissatisfied with this and in the following term I find myself grumbling about it, on May 31st, saying *It's a swizz going back so soon to school! Most schools had a week for Whitsun. We had two days for Whitsun AND* half term [i.e., combined]. *And we had prep!* It was probably harder for our staff than for us, though. They must have spent much of that February weekend marking papers, for some of them had results ready for us as soon as we got back.

Tuesday February 14 Mummy still on holiday. Jan and I went back. Algebra results. I was second with 84%. Geometry. First tie with Sonja 89%.

Went into every lesson with a beating heart but these were the only two results.

The beating heart might have been a ritualistic expression of nervousness as required by the schoolgirl code, mentioned above, but in my case I must admit it would have been a symptom of excitement rather than dread. I did well in exams without too much pain. Anticipation of the results was a pleasurable feeling. The strange thing was that as I look through the percentages recorded in the Diary I see that I did better in maths and science than in the humanities. *Arith results 91%. 2nd with Evelyn Cox. G.Peters top, 94%!* In history I came 8th with 73% and in English *5th with Diane and B. Wolf* with 70%. Yet at no point in my school career did it occur to me to become a scientist of any kind.

Apart from the mechanical aspects of physics, such as how to generate an electrical current, which did not much appeal to me even when demonstrated by pleasant Miss Lovelace, I liked the science subjects, especially biology, and was loath to give them up when the choice had to be made between 'Science' and 'Arts' for A Levels. I once asked in a chemistry lesson 'How do we know atoms exist if we can't see them?' and Miss Lacey promised it was something she would teach us later on. It made me quite glum to think of missing that when I had to drop the subject. But somehow the assumption had become established in the family that I was an Arts person. Maybe it arose because I was good at ART and had asserted since the age of about seven that I was going to be an artist when I grew up.

45

A prime objective in our exam system was to achieve a good average. You constantly totted up the marks as they came in and calculated your position in relation to your nearest rivals. Try as I might, I never beat our brainiest girl, Janet Barrell. She always came first and was, in fact, so outstanding that a term or so later she was moved up to the year above us. At one point we were neck and neck – *Average 83.8, Barrell's 86.5* – but geography brought my average down. I managed however to hang on to the vital target of having an 'honours average', in other words above 75%. The competitiveness was not simply a matter of jostling among ourselves. Our positions in class went down on our report and form prizes depended on it.

A constant source of pressure to succeed, for me, was the extended family's assumption that I was as good as my mother. It was taken for granted that I would follow in her footsteps and win a State Scholarship. Nowadays such expectations are regarded as a burden, but they were really only part and parcel of adult pride and confidence in a child and it was largely out of my pride in Mother that I imposed the obligation on myself. At the age thirteen I too took the future achievement for granted. I was not a dunce and it seemed a distant but definite goal to which all my school work was ultimately directed. I thought no further than that; I did not know where I would go or what I would do with the Scholarship and was not troubled at that stage by the conflict that would arise between university and art college. As the potential attainment came closer, however, I could see that it grew ever less likely and I tried to warn my nearest and dearest of the truth. 'I'm not going to get a State Scholarship, you know', I once said at a family gathering when I was about seventeen and I remember my Auntie Barbara in particular laughing at such a silly notion and declaring 'Of course you will!'

But I didn't.

That one black spot in my exam record in 1950, geography, was the one I had been 'dreading more than any'. *Failed in Geog 42%. Thought I would. 16th.* There was nothing intrinsic to geography that could cause this and I did not dislike the

46

subject. It was just an example of a failure to get along with the teacher. I could not please Miss Meir. I remember taking great care over my work for her and it used to puzzle me that I could not meet her standards. Until the Lower Fourth I had done perfectly well under other geography teachers; and other girls, whom until then I might have surpassed, were having no problem.

I wonder sometimes whether there were just one or two members of staff whom I encountered who, on account of my being known as a 'good girl' or a 'clever girl', were prejudiced against me from the start. Perhaps I transmitted an air of complacency and they were determined to bring me down a peg. At this distance in time, I cannot blame them in the slightest. I can on the other hand recall Miss Meir as a person of impenetrable coldness. That was the thing about her. She was totally unsmiling. She neither became angry nor did she try to expostulate over poor work nor help one to improve. I once left the join showing where my pencil had started and finished in tracing the outline of Australia. She incised a large red ring around it and the feeling was that my whole effort was quite worthless. The map and I were rejected. *I'm sure Miss Meir hates me* I wrote.

These recollections fill me with sympathy for those who go through their entire school lifetime under such circumstances: disliked and with no hope of doing any good.

* * * * *

When we were not having exams, we were having that lesser variation of them, 'tests', Latin tests being the commonest, but such rigours were balanced by lessons like these:
Wednesday February 22   Went for a nature walk in Biology period. Bird-watching. Saw and heard a skylark.
And on March 15:
Nature stroll of a different kind in Biology. Miss Cook showed us types of digging and how a compost heap is built up.
Both at school and at home, nature walks, sometimes solitary ones, had long been an established feature of life. On

47

one occasion, for instance: *Went for a long and thorough nature walk after breakfast. Filled 3 pages with notes.* In the wonderful garden at Wolsey Road I spent many purposeful hours following the pathways in order to scrutinise every familiar yard of the beds and borders for seasonal developments. Apparently the first crocus bloomed on February 3rd in 1950, and by the 18th the weather had taken a good stride towards Spring with *lots of mauve and orange crocuses, one miniature iris, one jonquil, two little snowdrops out.*

The next day there were primroses, and I was clearly ecstatic over the *glorious weather* which enabled us to build a *smashing camp* in the garden with the Fermor girls and to have tea out of doors, in the camp, *for the first time this year.*

In early March the weather was so fine that although I was away from school again with a cold, and merited supper in bed, I was not kept indoors. With Jan, home for her weekly half day (an indulgence enjoyed by LEH girls until they came into the main school), I played outside all the afternoon, and we saw *lots of large newts in pond. Caught three. Mating season. They'll breed soon. Wonderful weather and quite hot. Many flowers out. Fed hens with dandelions. Lots of cats about. It's just like the old summer evenings.*

No wonder we learned to love nature. That garden was an enchanted place. Everything about it was mature and mellow. Its lawns and beds had been laid down three score and ten years ago. Its trees were full of ancient wisdom and the old weathered stems of the climbing roses had grown almost as thick and stiff as their supporting posts, with thorns as blunt as thumbnails. Yet it was also vigorous. The roses sprouted an abundance of buds, the trees would produce crops of sweet, noble apples, and the pond was alive with newts and tadpoles.

As we looked out on the garden from the back door, we would see, lying immediately before us, the broad lawn where we could run and skip and chase, but the eye always seemed to be led towards the top right-hand corner and the serene little rustic structure of Rose Cottage, shaped like a circular haystack with a bench inside, our shelter and resting place, a den, a 'home', or simply a meeting centre where we sat on the bench and gossiped with Paul.

Behind it lay the wire-netted run and the shed where a dozen hens were kept. We used to go dashing up to the wire crying, 'Hens! Hens! Hens!', at which the silly clucking creatures would hurry stiffly to snatch at the handfuls of chickweed that we pushed through to them.

The pond was perhaps the richest source of interest in all the garden. In the summer months, Jan and I sometimes waited for hours squatting on the flat rocks at the water's edge to watch the emergence of a dragonfly. The brown crustaceous nymph would crawl slowly from the sediment up the stem of a water iris and there stay for almost a day while its skin opened and the lordly, glittering inner creature eased its way into the sunlight.

I am sorry to say that if hope of a good season ahead was implanted by that warm March, the promise was not fulfilled, for the old summer evenings did not return in their previous good measure. An official long-term weather forecast that I took note of proved accurate and 1950 turned into a rather wet year.

* * * * *

The Diary illustrates the fact that in school life there was hardly ever a time when lessons went on in a regular unbroken way. There was always some activity taking place which had to be accommodated. If one drew a graph, exams of course would loom as one of the largest peaks but there would be minor ups and downs for every outing, concert or play, largish ones for the major sports events, and every now and then some sizeable bump for one of the annual occasions of the school calendar. The Junior Prizegiving and the Gym Competition were the next high points of the graph for us in the spring term of 1950.

Preparations for Prize Day began on February 28th with our practising the songs we were to sing. *We're singing stupid songs!* I wrote and I know why we thought they were stupid: we considered they were too childish for us. Miss Maden made it

49

abundantly clear that we were by no means the mature people we perceived ourselves to be. We were juniors, still far down the school. Our own opinion was that we were juniors only nominally for the purposes of the Prizegiving, the prizes being those awards we had won in the previous academic year. Our dignity in the eyes of all the real juniors would be compromised. One of the songs was *John Cook* (lend me your grey mare, etc.) but I believe it was the other one which was the main bone of contention.

'*Good morrow, Mister Sailorman*' it went. '*I like your jolly smile*' or words to that effect. '*Where have you been since last we met, Old time a-bowling by?*

'*Singapore and Soo-oo-ez, all the places I don't know,*

'*And through the Bay of Biscaa-ay O! where the winds for ever blow*'.

A song so crass as to address itself to 'Mister Sailorman' in a hearty tune certainly deserves to be scorned by people of thirteen or any other age.

To spur us on in our melodious efforts, Miss Maden used the jocular cry of 'Come on now, you rabbits,' her deep voice taking on the accent of the blunt, bluff northerner which no doubt she was proud to be. She was a very firm woman of stocky build with curly white hair. Singing lessons were held in the hall and she would conduct from the platform with the class lined up before her as if on parade. We had to be on our feet with arms crossed behind our backs in order to expand our chests and breathe correctly. She was not a harsh person but she could be impatient and you had to jolly well get those songs right. Over and over again we'd go through them, bar by bar, word by word. Of all the staff's efforts, it would be her contribution to the production of well-educated girls that was the one most immediately on display on Prize Day. Every class had to sing. Excellence was demanded, as if of the chorus of the Royal Opera.

While Miss Maden's baton waved in front of us and our eyes were fixed upon it (to a degree that caused a sort of mesmeric effect and a bout of fainting fits at one stage), the accompaniment was being sustained by a very different sort of lady at the grand piano in the corner. Miss Morgan-Brown was exceedingly thin and her spine curved as though nature had shaped her for sitting bowed over a keyboard. Her face was so gaunt that it was skull-like and from it there issued a high, thin voice. She and Miss Maden shared a home in musical comradeliness and I sometimes wonder whether the former was greatly dominated by the latter. Occasionally Miss Maden's general impatience with all of us would wash over Miss M-B as well, so that she too became one of the class, as it were, a little flustered and hastening to play the tune as Miss Maden wished.

I cannot say I really knew either of these teachers at all well, neither, am I sure, did they know me. I wish I'd had the sense to see that it would one day be worth any amount of toil and moil to be able to play a musical instrument. I also wish I had joined the school choir. Unfortunately, as I have already mentioned, my musical education had been abandoned in earlier years. I had had one piano teacher who was a dragon and who rapped my knuckles with a ruler and one who was a mouse, too gentle to enforce the practising. Like Baby Bear's porridge, Miss Morgan-Brown might well have proved the in-between who was just right, but she was not to have the opportunity of demonstrating this. No doubt there was some thought of not throwing further fees down the drain on my behalf.

* * * * *

We were thoroughly drilled for Prize Day, rehearsing not only our songs but our entry into the hall, our seating and our manner of receiving prizes. Prizewinners had to leave their places and line up by the platform in batches of six or eight at a time ready to march up the steps and across the stage to the VIP who was making the presentations. We had to step out pretty briskly, for neither the VIP nor parents would want to drag the thing on longer than necessary. The latter would each be faced with about half an hour's continuous polite applause of other people's daughters for the sake of their own ewe lamb's few seconds of glory. We needed also to sense which foot to turn on to make a curtsey (I *think* we curtsied to all prize presenters, not only the titled ones) and to accomplish it without appearing too militarily rigid. Then we had to come down from the platform on the far side with decent haste while the next girl was making her way up.

The platform would be crowded with governors, the table in the centre stacked with books and trophies, and the body of the hall packed with girls, teachers, mothers and fathers. The gallery too was full of parents. The staff all wore their academic gowns. The reason why we Lower Fourths had to be included in the Junior Prizegiving, singing inappropriate songs, even though we were by then in our second year in the main school, was that it would have been impossible to cram us in with the seniors. We sat in our tight rows and were supposed not to look round to seek out or signal to our own people.

Regarding the prizes themselves, we had the freedom to choose our own books to a given value according to the nature of the prize. The school then purchased them, stamped them on the cover with the crest in gold leaf and pasted a label on the inside recording the details, endorsed by the headmistress's signature. The books I chose that term were *Art through the Ages,* and *The Summer of the Great Secret.* The last was simply a story book I had heard well of from somebody, but I regretted having chosen it. I don't think I bothered to read it.

The titled luminaries referred to above would have been the preserve of the seniors' function. Our guest of honour presenting the prizes in 1950 was not quite so illustrious, being Mrs Geard, wife of a former Chairman of the Governors. One day before the great occasion itself Mrs Geard visited the school and was shown round. The perfectly normal interest she displayed in the school's minor attractions evidently struck me at the time as strange, and the poor woman has been branded in the record as an oddity ever since: *Mrs Geard, who will be presenting our prizes, came in with Miss Scott and, presumably, Mr Geard. This was in P.S.* [Private Study]. *Of all queer things, they came to see the guinea pigs in the Bio. Lab!*

The whole ritual of the great event invariably passed

smoothly and well it might, considering how many lessons we had missed in order to rehearse. Indeed, in view of the total time taken up by functions such as Prizegiving (including the entire day itself when we came to school only for the ceremony at about 3.0 p.m.) and in general by lessons lost through absence of staff or children, by a whole week and more given over to exams, and by afternoons spent watching matches, hearing election results or being shown films – I find it hard to see, in view of all this, what time we had left for ordinary old learning.

* * * * *

If there was one subject which, even more than Geography, should have taught me humility, it was P.T. There were two sorts of P.T. lessons: games and 'gym'.

In games I was just not very good. All through the summer of 1950 I recorded a growing passion for tennis, but alas it is not true that you like what you are good at and are good at what you like. Nothing, not all the practice and passion in the world, could have made me into a decent tennis player. As for lacrosse in the winter and autumn terms, it was abysmal. The only things I could manage reasonably well were scoring goals in netball and hitting the ball in rounders. I suppose I had a fairly good eye and could aim straight. Besides, you don't actually have to be moving very fast while engaged in either of those two actions, so they were relatively easy to accomplish. I was not good at throwing but the motion of putting a netball through its ring is more like lifting or tossing.

As a fielder in rounders, I was so scared of the hard ball flying at me and so scared of running to catch it in case of crashing into a fellow fielder rushing after the same shot, each of us with our eyes fixed high on the ball in the air and not seeing one another, that I was a complete butter-fingers of a catcher.

In lacrosse too it was mainly fear that inhibited me. To play lacrosse wholeheartedly you have to be able to hurl yourself around, to duck and weave and to plunge through a mob of flailing sticks, cradling the ball in your own stick and not be afraid of either being hurt or hurting other players. It was Pauline Dacombe, I think, who had her front teeth knocked out one day in the mêlée. It seemed to me to be a horrific price to pay for playing a game and it reinforced my wonderment as to how other girls could abandon themselves so to the physical rough and tumble and not mind all that much about the bruises. But then other girls could deliberately create a slide on a stretch of icy pavement and apparently not think about whether they might fall.

It was in the gymnasium above all, however, that my fear came out and it was fear of a different kind from that of the games field. It is revealed in the Diary only indirectly to begin with. Follow this curious tale of terror:

Monday January 16 P.T. in afternoon. Can do a handstand and somersault against bar!

(So far so good; a brave effort though hardly a remarkable achievement for a thirteen-year-old.)

Friday January 27 Gym second thing. I don't mind doing sommersaults so much now.

But a couple of weeks later the brave act began to break down:

Monday January 20 Practising for the Gym competition. We've got to do those somersaults!

Friday March 10 Had last Gym lesson before competition. Faye and I are dreading it.

At this point the panic had reached its peak, but some sort of moral stiffening seems to have taken place thereafter, which I hope was shared by Faye and any other timorous classmates of our ilk, because at a Gym Competition rehearsal in the lunch hour on March 13th I could *almost do those somersaults, thank goodness!*

Finally, after one more lunch hour rehearsal which was 'quite nice', we came to the real thing on Friday the 17th:

Watched X's (our sister form, Lower IV X) *competition then had our own try. Miss Morton judged, all went very quickly but am glad there's not another Gym competition for a year.* It was those rivals of ours, the X's, who won the Lower School Cup.

The fact was that I could have been forced round an ice rink or ordered to stand in goal before an entire hail of lacrosse balls as hard as granite and it would not have charged me with the same sickening reluctance as going head over heels. Whichever way you spell it, a somersault entails turning upside down. At some point in its execution you are going to find yourself with your heels higher than your head and this was what I could not bear.

Even the sort of exercises which are performed lying flat on a mat on the floor of the gymnasium were unpleasant to me. The ceiling above was so high that as you lay there you could not be sure your body was on the level. You only had to be asked to point your feet in the air and your whole balance felt wrongly tilted. I used to try to hold on to the ground by pressing the palms of my hands as hard as I could on the floor

The Gym. Photograph 1955 Note the sturdy grey knickers!

55

on either side of me. It was not the height of the room in itself that was the source of the problem but the upsetting of my horizontal axis, as witness the fact that I would cheerfully have climbed the ropes to the very top.

Perversely enough, climbing the ropes, among other feats that appealed to me, was something I was incapable of doing. I tried it many times. I would confidently haul myself up the first few feet, hand over hand, knees and ankles clenched on the rope and then, unable to keep my grip, would slither back down to the ground. So I was caught between what I wanted to do but could not and what I could have done but would not. Altogether I made a sorry gymnast.

The only reason for my ever managing to do a handstand or somersault was, I believe, the patience of our kind young gym mistress for that year, Miss Miller, who coaxed and encouraged even the most athletically resistant children.

* * * * *

They hadn't coined the word 'shopaholic' in 1950 but through the Diary can be seen the budding of a later passion. Even more regular than the school timetable was the main household duty that I performed each week, which was the shopping. It usually consisted of two journeys along Bridge Road, one for the greengrocery, the heaviest load, and one for all the rest.

From the age of six, I had been sent to 'just pop up the shops' and by the time I was seven shopping was established as my special task. It was willingly done, I'm certain of that, otherwise I'd have worn Mother down, complaining about it.

As soon as I visualise stepping up (two high steps from street level) into the doorway of the greengrocer's, a vivid picture is evoked of the pictorial contrast between the glossy yellows, reds and greens of fruit and salads and the dry brown dustiness of the floorboards, boxes and sacks, ingrained with the mud constantly brought in with the root vegetables. Three middle-aged sisters named Starkey, always wearing blue overalls, ran the shop. My shopping list usually began with four pounds of potatoes and was bound to include some of the greens that

Mother adored and we girls detested. Fresh fruit was seen as a necessity, not a luxury, despite occasional exclamations from Auntie Kathleen about the extravagance.

Having carried home two bags full of our extravagances, I set off again to deal with the butcher, the baker, the chemist, the ironmonger and the sweet shop. The grocer, I believe, delivered an order once a week.

The sweet shop was reserved till last, sometimes indeed being dignified by a third journey after the mundane necessities were done, in which case Jan and I would generally go tripping round there together, untrammelled by any other burdens than some cash and our ration books. We called it simply The White Shop and the proprietor was, as I remember, a rather burly chap in a brown overall.

On April 22nd I went to collect our new ration books, to last us the year presumably. The existence of rationing through almost our entire life as a family had led to a system of individual choice over the consumption of the two most prized commodities, sweets and butter. Three dishes in the kitchen cupboard held our separate butter portions for the week so that we could be thrifty or lavish with it according to temperament, always facing the prospect of being reduced to margarine in the end – and margarine in those days bore no resemblance to its relatively palatable modern descendants. Every few weeks the longing for more butter would impel us to churn some for ourselves. This meant saving the top of the milk for several days and shaking it for hours in a jam jar. Each of us would shake in turn until her arms ached, a chore that was less boring than it sounds because it was so satisfying to see the butter solidify.

The same principle of portioning things out applied to sweets, along with the added benefit that each of us could choose her own varieties. Long after rationing ceased, we still purchased sweets in tiny amounts, two ounces of this and two ounces of that and the total quantity remained moderate, for whether they were to be gorged in one go or nibbled at singly, lingeringly, the proper time for this procedure was only after tea. There came a time when this rule had to be

57

officially overturned, but this occurrence will be explained later.

Close to the White Shop the most enticing place in the street (to me) presented its dignified dark green exterior to the public. It was Taylors' the newsagents. Mr and Mrs Taylor were not only newsagents, however. They also sold stationery and books and consequently it was into their till that the major portion of my pocket money jingled. Pencils, inks, crayons, notepads, exercise books, paint brushes, poster paints and drawing paper were the tools and raw materials of creation for Jan and me. Long ago, during the War, Mummy had been advised to buy if she possibly could something more generous for us to paint on than the standard little children's drawing books then obtainable. I had learned therefore to ask for 'A sheet of drawing paper, please', which for fourpence procured me a large piece of decent cartridge paper in the old imperial size, which even when folded into four allowed for artistic composition on a spacious scale.

I think it must have been from Taylors that I bought my Diary.

* * * * *

Saturday March 4 Have saved 12/- for Jan's birthday, etc. Latin with Colonel Gettins.

Tuesday March 7 Away from school with a cold. Did some Latin and lots of painting. Painted pictures for Latin nursery rhymes.

Saturday March 11 Got shopping done early but could not go to Latin as Colonel was busy.

Our first foreign language lessons at LEH were French, which began as soon as we entered the main school. Latin started one year later and I think it was at least another year before girls who had decided to develop their modern languages could take up German. I was destined to stay a classicist and perhaps the foundations of that choice were partly laid by Colonel Gettins.

I believe the Colonel was fond of me and, had I had a

58

modern child's freedom from the formality of behaviour in those days towards adults, I might have shown him the affection of a surrogate granddaughter. As it was, he directed his attention to the improvement of my mind. This I remember to have been the devoted aim of many of the elders around me and the Colonel's contribution was to offer Latin coaching. He was particularly keen to know how I got on in this subject, dear to his heart, and it pleased him to see that I took to it well.

As soon as I had acquired some basic knowledge I was ready to present myself at his study on Saturday mornings, after the shopping, for half an hour or so. His teaching system was simple and unusual. All I did was to learn nursery rhymes.

Tini, tini, tini, felis est in puteo ...
Mariae agnellus erat ...
Cara felis, cara felis, unde domum redis?...

One of the Latin nursery rhymes

59

The Colonel had produced these translations many years before, for the benefit of his own sons, I think. They were wonderful. My private tuition continued for only a few months but in that time *Pippa Bella parva, Jacobus Juliaque, Parvus Willi-Winkie* and the *Mures Caeci tres* helped to introduce all kinds of syntax and vocabulary in a most memorable fashion. Some words were untranslatable of course, but who could forget the Latin for 'sheep' after learning '*Baa baa, ovis negra*'?

* * * * *

The buying of food and eating it were matters dwelt on the Diary but the intermediate process of cooking it received scant attention. I was not the sort of girl to hang around the kitchen, eager to join in whatever Mummy was doing, though of course by the age of thirteen I had to help when required and could rustle up a cooked snack if necessary. My contributions to meals more often took the form of laying and clearing the table and washing and drying up. The theme of food, however, comes through patently and repeatedly.

Sunday March 12   Went to Pam's for day ... had tea in their lounge. Merangues, éclairs!

Friday March 31   Mummy home about 3.30 p.m. Had a small snack tea. Went off about 10 to 5. Gag met us. Had big tea (tinned plums, bananas, Libby's milk) when there.

A couple of days later: *Have eaten all Gag's bananas and apples.*

Tuesday April 4   Went to Kingston with Mummy after lunch. This was a long-promised treat. Snack tea in Zeeta's. I had 1 éclaire, 2 meringues, and one other cake.

Monday May 1   Jan's birthday. ... Paul to tea. Mushrooms, iced biscuits, fizzy pop.

And apart from these gala menus, there are brief entries of other meals deemed worth a mention, from the simple *beans for tea* to *Lovely lunch – blackcurrants!* or *We had a lovely pudding – blancmange and ice cream!*

Our main meal of the day was lunch, referred to as lunch apparently rather than 'dinner' even at school, a discovery from the Diary that surprised me. The later meal was tea, meaning high tea, something like beans or spaghetti on toast (tinned spaghetti, naturally – we'd never heard of 'pasta'), cold meat, ham, corned beef, kippers or other fish, scrambled egg or occasionally bacon. It would also include the ingredients of afternoon tea – bread and butter, jam, sandwich spread, biscuits, cakes and buns. The day was rounded off for Jan and me with a light supper after our bath or wash, a snug and relaxing little snack, typically half an apple, half an orange and half a bag of crisps, savoured and prolonged as one sat curled up in the fireside armchair, eyes on a book, delaying the call to bed.

Despite such commodities as bacon and eggs appearing regularly on the teatime menu, the Diary shows that we ate bacon for breakfast as well, at least, on the evidence of the only mention of it, one Sunday in July: I had got up late and *I decided to cook breakfast myself. Bacon was a bit burnt but the tomatoes were fine.* It has become an article of faith that 'everyone ate a cooked breakfast in those days', but how did the limited rations of bacon stretch to it and how, even if there were enough, was repetition avoided between breakfast and tea? There were cereals and toast, of course, but I doubt if they alone would have constituted a 'proper' meal to go forth on for the day.

The school lunch on nine days out of ten was based upon the archetypal balanced main meal: meat, potato and a vegetable. The meat was either sliced roast lamb or beef, mince, mutton, stew or cold meats – the latter, as at home, varying from corned beef, spam or luncheon meat to cold roasts. The potatoes were boiled or mashed, but roasted once a year with our Christmas turkey. Chicken was still a luxury meat, equivalent to turkey, and did not appear on the school menu. The vegetables were usually carrots, peas, beans, greens or swede. Sprouts perhaps made an occasional appearance but probably gave the staff so much trouble in persuading children to eat them (though theoretically we had no choice) and the cooks so much irritation due to the amounts wasted, that I daresay they were considered an unwise option. Broccoli, peppers and courgettes were unknown to us.

Two or three times a term we were given the one guaranteed, universal plate-clearing combination: sausage and chips. First helpings would be tipped out on to plates around each table at racing speed while the table monitresses stood by quivering to snatch the serving dishes and rush to the hatch for seconds. A third helping, won by those lucky sprinters who made the final dash before supplies ran out, vanished as fast as the first.

Puddings were utterly orthodox, obeying every precept as to what school puddings ought to be. Anyone from that era could reel off the same list – spotted dick, jam roly-poly, semolina, stewed fruit, chocolate sponge, and so forth. Custard came with most things.

It is of course *de rigeur* to complain about school dinners but I must admit that, so long as I was not forced to eat cabbage and provided there was enough crab-apple jelly to disguise the milk puddings, I found the food palatable. The only problem was the one immortalised by Olive Twist. Catering probably had to be done within very tight limits and the meals could not quite fill you up, so there had to be some means to alleviate the widespread malaise of constant peckishness among growing girls. For anyone not too choosy, plain semolina, devoid of jam or crab-apple jelly, was available every day as a second pudding. Sometimes the semolina was brown, which unfortunately did not mean it contained chocolate or other flavouring – it was just brown semolina! However, there was a more palatable alternative. Two innovations had been introduced to the school in the late 1940s. One took the form of a trolley-load of buns, wheeled into the hall at morning break time to be sold for a penny each, and the other was even better: Wall's ice cream in threepenny blocks. These were to be had only once a week, though, as a Friday treat. Such extras, which in some schools would have been called 'tuck', merely supplemented the biscuits which most of us carried in our satchels in any case as a snack for our morning break.

Unexpectedly, I find from the Diary that it was not compulsory to drink the free school milk. It must have felt all the more virtuous therefore to do so voluntarily. This November entry: *Had milk at recess for the second or third time this term!* almost has a halo inscribed over it.

It was a relief to my mother that on reaching my teens I had developed a large appetite. Until then I had been a finicky little girl. Insatiable hunger was the hallmark of the normal adolescent growth spurt. It gratified her to observe my Billy Bunterish consumption of buns and meringues and to hear, within two hours of any meal, renewed cries of, 'I'm *starving!*'

Jan came out even better than I did in this respect. She was diagnosed by the school doctor as having a quick metabolism, which required an instant ingestion of sweets when she arrived home from school. This brilliant medical coup overrode all previous rules about when and how sweets could be eaten.

* * * * *

The arrangements made by the school for six hundred girls and perhaps forty staff to enjoy a midday meal entailed far more than simply cooking and dishing up the food. There was no permanent refectory at LEH, a sad deficiency in a building not even as old as I was. The kitchens had been sited adjacent to the assembly hall. As a result, the hall's parquet floor was subjected daily to the setting up of rows and rows of folding tables, an operation using much of Mr Rayner the caretaker's time, and its fine wall panelling, like false bookshelves concealing a secret passage, had to be opened to reveal two wide serving hatches.

The juniors from Burlington House were marched over the field to take the first sitting and their meals were presented to them ready as a plateful, the plates being stacked with metal rings between them. It was these young ones in whom any failure to eat up all they were given was therefore evident. We seniors of the main school were allowed to help ourselves from oval aluminium vegetable dishes.

There must have been eleven girls at every table, two from each year and a head of table who was a Lower Sixth former. We retained the same places for the whole school year. The pair of Upper Fourths were always the waitresses to their table, fetching and carrying the dishes. They were the ones who had to run for extra chips. At the back of the hall, beneath the gallery, four or five tables were set up for girls from all years who for various reasons brought their own packed lunches.

Two mistresses sat on the platform, side by side, eating their own food while facing out over the chattering, clattering sea of girls. One of the two would say grace: 'For what we are about to receive may the Lord make us truly thankful. Amen'. Then hundreds of chairs would scrape the parquet and the whole noisy business would begin. There was no ban on talking during the meal.

One or two of the cooks might emerge from the kitchen, wheeling trolleys, mopping up, helping generally, but there were no 'dinner ladies' as such. The nearest thing to a dinner lady was the school caterer cum matron, Miss Broughton, who walked between the ranks of tables hoping to see that the nutrition so carefully planned by her was being consumed.

The ever-expanding population of LEH meant that yet another of its best rooms was disrupted and infected by cabbagy smells, for the staff, apart from the two on duty, dined in the library. Meanwhile, the Upper Sixth, released briefly from the onus of keeping other people in order, had a corner to themselves at the end of a corridor.

* * * * *

'You're mad. You'll pay for this when you are sixty', said Doctor Bowling, our family doctor, to my mother, but seeing how determined she was he signed the form in front of him. It was the summer of 1949 and he was the final obstacle which she had to break through in order to be admitted to the training course. The first doctor who had examined her, the man from the Ministry appointed to conduct medicals of all the would-be teachers, had rejected her immediately. He had detected the murmur of the mitral valvular heart disease which she had suffered since childhood.

Mother had been twelve years old when this condition was first found and it was attributed to some earlier undiagnosed attack of rheumatic fever. She was promptly put to bed for six months and her parents were told that she should never again be allowed to take part in any sport, nor must she try to swim, nor even run for a bus. She spent most of her subsequent school games lessons usefully and contentedly employed as an umpire without ever playing, but this limitation was for many years the sole recognition of the problem. There seem to have been no further attempts at treatment or investigation and, even in childbearing, no special care.

It was another matter, however, to undertake the taxing profession of teaching, and Mother had a fight on her hands. The medical officer from the Ministry of Health had demanded, when he turned her down, 'Could you walk round Bushy Park?'

'Yes!' she replied, and he said 'You are lying, aren't you?'

Nevertheless, she was so persistent that he sought reinforcements, referring her to a panel of other doctors who unanimously backed up their colleague and declared Mother's state of health not fit enough for teaching. What she then said and how she persuaded them I do not know, but somehow the flat refusal turned into a concession that if she obtained the permission of her own family doctor, they would accept her. Hence the consultation with Dr Bowling, who lived next door to us at number five Wolsey Road, and his long-term warning. I can imagine each of those well-meaning MDs sighing resignedly as they passed this unreasonable woman on for somebody else to cope with.

Paying the price of her perversity when she was sixty must have seemed a remote threat, for Mother was only thirty four when this happened, though in a way she paid the price constantly throughout her working years, in terms of fatigue. In addition, her determination had the unforeseen side effect that whenever she needed to obtain a certificate from Dr Bowling for flu or any minor ailment, he always sent her back to work within the shortest possible time. No doubt he perceived her as a woman passionate for her career and would have had little idea of the rigours of that career. Many and many a time she longed for another day or two of rest, yet never dreamed of arguing with his verdicts and so returned to the classroom still half worn out. Nearly thirty years were to pass before a different doctor in a different place suggested medication and regular examinations to improve her heart condition.

During the especially gruelling year of teacher training, it was frequently remarked in the Diary that Mummy was 'very tired'. However, she came through it to be acclaimed the most outstanding student of her year and to become a much sought after and prized teacher, and well into her old age she regularly walked round Bushy Park.

* * * * *

In other ways too 1950 was a year of hardship. It was perhaps our poorest year, with Mummy not earning, yet having to pay Shoo. We lived entirely upon the maintenance paid by my father which was, I believe, quite generous but reduced by almost half due to taxation. In those days, married women – and Mother was still married, legally separated but not divorced – were entitled to no tax allowance of their own. Even worse was that with dreadful injustice (corrected presumably by the time broken families became more common) my father's payments were treated as 'unearned income', taxable at the highest rate, a concept which inflicted a further deprivation upon us because it barred Mother from receiving any kind of grant while at college. Thrown into the same category as the possessors of stocks and shares and other forms of invested wealth, the person living on 'unearned income' was deemed to be seated comfortably on a fat cushion of capital.

Mother was one of only two students in her year at Hampton College who were refused a grant and the other was a woman who acknowledged herself to be in no need of one since she was supported by a prosperous husband. A further iniquity was committed when Mother took up her first teaching post in September 1950. One of the inducements of the emergency training scheme was that increments to their starting salaries were promised to the recruits, to be based on their previous employment. Admittedly Mother's other jobs, apart from running a home, had all been rather humble (clerical work) or rather informal (assisting a family friend, a child psychiatrist, as what would now be called a psychiatric social worker). Yet when a fellow student from Hampton could successfully claim the increment on the grounds of having worked in a sweet shop, it is not easy to see why Mother was denied it. She trudged into Kingston on many Saturday mornings to plead her case at County Hall but gave up eventually from exhaustion.

If Dr Bowling could only have known it, the driving force that kept Mother going through the struggle was not ambition for professional achievement but the will to raise us to a better life. For all her intelligence and scholastic success, she was not a career woman. Given that she had to work, teaching was an enduring and worthy occupation and the thing she loved best, but she used to say it could never be her first choice. That place was held by the role she had lost at separation: as a housewife.

One of the pillars of our upbringing was that every generation must start life a step higher than the one before. Both our parents set out in the beginning aglow with the hope of a future far brighter for their children than their own childhoods had been. Jan and I knew our education was part of those aspirations. Mother was now restarting the climb on her own. We understood. The bone-scraping frugality of life in the flat would one day lead to a house of our own, with a bedroom each. A golden age would come.

3

DEATH AND BIRTH

The Easter holiday in 1950 lasted from 23rd March till 19th April, a period of nearly four weeks in which the engrossing concerns of our life shifted, naturally enough, from school to family. It was marked by a death and a birth and by our flowing together again for a while in the old living river with Nanny and Gagga, with all our maternal uncles, aunts and cousins, and with great aunts.

The death came first, on 24th March, when the Diary states: *Auntie Margaret died early this morning. God Bless Her.*

Margaret Emily Jones, aged 76, was Gagga's eldest sister and had been ill for many months, dying from a secondary carcinoma of the liver. Although for years she had lived in Torquay with Auntie May, their other sister, when taken ill she had been brought to Hayes. Possibly Gagga decided that owing to his position as secretary at the Cottage Hospital he could procure the best nursing care. He had taken me there to see her once, just after Christmas, and Matron had led us towards Auntie Margaret's bed in a long ward, pausing on the way to bend down towards me and whisper gently, 'You understand that your Auntie won't look the same as when you last saw her? She is very ill.' I nodded mutely. In fact, we went no closer than a yard or two from the end of the bed. Auntie Margaret was asleep. I looked at her for a few moments. She was turned on her side and I could hardly even make out the features of the white face on the pillow.

I have no memory of Auntie Margaret as anything other than pale and quiet. A thumbnail character sketch would be composed of the above instance and a few other fleeting

68

impressions; for instance, a recollection of entering a room in the house in Torquay, on my own, and playing on the floor, talking to myself, before realising that Auntie Margaret was seated in the wing chair, thin, upright and still, watching me. This epitomised the way I perceived her – as a figure in the background.

During another Torquay holiday, another Easter, she and Auntie May had each invited the three of us to visit their respective places of worship. Bustling, talkative, buxom Auntie May with her flamboyant hats and passion for clothes, had taken us on Good Friday to her utterly unadorned, nonconformist chapel. Then on the Sunday we had gone with reserved and reticent Auntie Margaret and had feasted our senses on the incense, the organ music and the triumphant processional richness of a full High Anglican Easter morning service.

The death certificate, in the column headed Occupation, describes her as 'spinster' and 'independent' but, when young, Margaret had worked as a milliner, displaying the flare for design that came out in her generation of the Joneses.

* * * * *

On a Friday afternoon eight days after the end of the Lady Eleanor Holles term, Hampton College broke up and we went immediately over to Cambria. The journey used to take about one and a half hours on three buses, first the 201 to Feltham, then the 90B to Hayes, and finally the 607 trolleybus for the last mile, to Hayes End. It was often a dismal ride, in either direction, especially in the winter dark, with the waiting, the cold dim lights of the bus trundling towards you at last, and the drear comfort of the chilly interior after standing at the stop. On dark days or brighter ones, however, I could gaze out of the window and fall into the sort of daydreaming state that in any form of travel, whether by bus, train or car, was my chief pleasure.

The 90B portion of the journey was notable for the fact that it included a stretch of straight open lane across the flat Middlesex countryside which we knew was in the process of being turned into an airport. To us it was a nameless bit of land, but there had been an aerodrome there from before the War, with a village close by called Heath Row.

Sometimes Gagga met us in his car at the Corinth, the cinema which was the landmark called out by bus conductors at that particular stop. This eliminated the third bus ride and the culminating walk down the road to Cambria.

Cambria

Cambria was one of an estate of semi-detached three-bedroom houses, but because of its commanding position as the corner house, at a broad crossroads, it was larger than the rest. The front door stood under a substantial brick pillared porch, the hall was a square rather than the usual narrow passage and the staircase rose from it, not in sweeping grandeur exactly, but with a sort of solid oaken dignity, taking two bends upwards to the wide landing above. That staircase with its plain dark wooden banisters and square newel posts formed such a central feature of the house that it is the first thing that comes to mind when I picture Cambria. True to form, that weekend in 1950 it bore the scrambling up and down of us children like a great animal with cubs as Jan and I *played trains on stairs with Chris and Steven.*

The kitchen and the 'lounge' were larger than the average, too, which was just as well, because all extra space was needed for the Jones family's regular assemblies.

The builder of the estate, a man called de Salis, had had a reputation for building sound, solid houses and for caring about the welfare of his tenants. Apparently he had invited their comments and criticisms after they first moved in, in order to make improvements for the future. Nanny had told him the kitchen sink was too low.

There was one section of the Jones family that had no need to assemble at Cambria for they were already more or less on the doorstep. Barely fifty paces along the road, in another de Salis house, lived Auntie Ollie and Uncle Yoka and their two boys, Chris and Steven. Chris was almost exactly the same age as Jan and would soon be ten, while Steven was coming up to six. He had been born on D-Day.

Ollie was Olwen, Mother's sister. Strictly speaking, they were Richardses, not Joneses, but then we were Applebys. It made no difference. We belonged to the same great, spreading pyramid that had Nanny and Gagga at its pinnacle.

'Yoka' or 'Yok' was a variant of Jock,

Olwen, Yoka and their three boys. 1951

71

derived from Jack, the latter then being not a name in its own right as it has since become, but that to which most of the country's 'John' population answered if born before the Second World War. Gagga was in fact another Jack, though often addressed as Alfred (his second name) by his siblings, and in addition to these two we had Uncle John, Mother's youngest brother, who remained 'John', and a great-uncle Jack. Possibly in many families the alternation of John and Jack was a way of distinguishing between fathers, sons and brothers when there was certain to be at least one John in every generation.

Saturday April 1   Had breakfast in bed. Nan's eiderdowns have been covered with pink silk. Did some drawing. Cambridge won Boat Race. Plenty of April Fool tricks being done. Went shopping with Gag in afternoon. Went to see Oly's baby clothes.

The baby clothes would have been the layette prepared by Ollie for her third child, who was to be born before the Easter holiday was over.

Breakfast in bed usually meant in Nan's bed, with her spoiling us. It was a time-honoured custom that lasted until we were gawky great girls, to go clambering in with her and dip into the blue tin of biscuits they always kept by the bed. Gagga was usually the one to go down and fetch their cup of tea and then to go down again and get the breakfast started. Jan and I would be snuggling up to Nan and coaxing her to tell us for the hundredth time the story of The Little Girl who went to Fairyland. (More of this later.)

Whenever possible, the Joneses took the process of getting up in the morning at a leisurely pace and, if several scions of the family were staying at Cambria, a discussion could well begin at the breakfast table that would be on full throttle as the adults lit their cigarettes and barely be brought to a halt by Blondie, the next door neighbour, popping round for something. It would be eleven o'clock and we would all still be in our dressing gowns.

We spent only two nights at Cambria on this occasion but would be back within a few days. I think Mummy badly needed the support of her parents and brothers and sister and was probably longing to see them again after the long term, which made all the to-ing and fro-ing worth the trouble. Besides, this weekend would have been her only chance to spend any length of time among them, for while Jan and I were to have ten more days with our kith and kin, she herself was going away separately.

Mummy had hair done I wrote on 6th April, *ready for 'Paris au Printemps.'*

Auntie Kathleen was taking her to France.

Although it says nothing in the Diary except that she went back home after seeing us settled at Cambria on 7th April, I remember our making a tremendous, silly fuss about saying goodbye to her for our short interlude. Still, this no doubt pleased her far more than if we had just uttered a casual ''bye'.

Meanwhile, Cambria was filling up with the arrival of Uncle Ken, Auntie Barbara and our two little cousins, Vivien and Adrian, who were about five and three years old at this time. There was also a visit during the next two days from Uncle Mansell, though no mention in the Diary of whether Auntie Kitty had come with him. Kitty was subject to bouts of depression. If only she could manage to make the effort to get there, she was good company, would always produce her share of jokes and comic stories and was thoroughly one of the crowd. In her younger days she had ridden motor cycles round the Wall of Death, a career which you would think went with an adventurous personality. Yet now it was all too often beyond poor Mansell's powers to persuade her to drive up with him from Southend.

At any rate, whether accompanied or not by spouses, all the sons and daughters of Jack and Nellie Jones passed through the parental halls that Easter weekend: Mansell, the eldest, Kenneth, Valmai (Mother), Olwen and John.

Olwen's new baby would make the seventh grandchild. The three generations formed the shape of the family, as I saw it, each layer wider than the one above it. My own place was very clear: if it were all set out on a sheet of paper, I would be at the left hand end of the bottom line. Never mind that Ken was older than my mother and his children would have taken

73

L to R: Mother, Olwen, Mansell, John, Ken. 1954

precedence in any normal line of succession. No, I was the eldest grandchild, the firstborn, and the cousins were like my younger brothers and sisters. This was extremely important to me, so deeply planted were we in this maternal organism, the Family.

A very similar pyramid existed on our Appleby side, where again I was the first of my generation, but Jan and I had seen nothing of our paternal aunts and uncles and our Granny since the War and many years were to pass before our contact with them was restored.

* * * * *

Gagga sits at the green-chenille-covered dining room table, writing, a heavy amber coloured glass ash tray in front of him.

74

Gagga in 1949

His hair is pure white, he is wearing his glasses. Concentration makes him look stern, the folds of his flesh down the sides of his face deepened by the bend of his head over the paper. He works on in spite of the fact that people are coming in and out of the room, chatting, and children are dashing past him every couple of minutes. He is writing letters or working on business papers. Soon he will break off, remove his glasses, go through to the lounge and start talking to Mansell, because the table must be laid for lunch.

In 1900, acting, singing and poetry were in the blood of John Alfred Jones, and he came up from Carmarthen with romantic intentions of going on the London stage. His fine voice with its slight Welsh lilt seemed made for declaiming. Ten years later he was behind an office desk in the accounts office of a margarine factory in Southall and the prime years of his working life through the 1920s and '30s were shadowed by the Depression. But he'd met Nellie Syms and it was she, I would say, and religion, that have absorbed most of his romantic energies since then.

She, to us children, is our mild, soft little Nan, who never puts her teeth in except to go out and whose fingers for ever fidget restlessly on the arm of her chair. She also hums to herself and gives out sing-song snippets of lines about what she is doing; you hear a little tuneless trill – 'Half a pound of margarine' – as she weighs out ingredients.

There is a spirit of merriment in her though. We can tease

75

her or play tricks, sometimes making her jump out of her skin, and she loves it. She will chuckle or grin at us with a little hunch of her shoulders, and exclaim delightedly: 'Ooh, you wicked monkeys!'

Like her, Gagga has a regular story that he tells us. It is of a little boy in Wales who was sent by his mother to fetch milk from the nearby farm and on the way he suddenly saw a wonderful sight – the hunt rode by. Gagga forms a rounded fist through which he blows Ta-ra-ta-ra calls of the hunting horn and then, after a vivid account of the colours and the action, the story always finishes with the same formula: 'But all at once he trod on a pin, and the pin bended and the story ended'.

Gagga is deeply religious and his ardent mind has taken him on a perpetual quest. From the chapel in Wales, he joined the Plymouth Brethren on meeting Nan and over the next twenty years or so he went from one sect to another, seeking the one that would satisfy his soul. Finally he joined a tiny group called the Apostolic Faith Church, founded and run by a single family, one Pastor Dennis and his sons, promoting missionary work in Africa but operating at only one chapel in this country, in Bournemouth. Gagga himself is one of their pastors now, Pastor Jones, and this is the reason why he frequently goes down to Bournemouth and why the family has spent many holidays there.

Gagga has bequeathed to his children and his children's children an abiding precept: that on the great issues such as religion and politics, each person must form his or her own opinion. Thus despite his own strong beliefs he has never disputed the rights of his sons and daughters to go their own ways. This has resulted in every shade of thought being represented among the five of them, from a faith as fervent as his own to an equally sincere atheism.

Nan has been the steady one, I think, through thick and thin. The gift that she has is for simply going on with things whatever happens. Rich or poor, I imagine she has always been the same: self-effacing, worried, gentle, never toughened by the hard times of her life, never in control of her life either, but not remotely crushed on that account. By being her own quiet, diffident self she is respected, deferred to, watched over and loved.

* * * * *

Saturday April 8 Mummy left for France early in the morning. We slept in Nan's bed. Gag's at Bournemouth. Went to Hayes, got sweets. Went to rec' [the recreation ground across the road] *this afternoon with little ones. Olwen's baby due but was not born.*

Nanny in 1954

Sunday April 9 Wrote 3½ pages to Mummy. Mansell swindled us with his 'tests'. Chris and Steven, Auntie Barbara, Vivien, Adrian, Jan and I went over the rec'. Packed up after lunch. Drove off to Guildford. Ken's got a T.V. We were home in time to watch.

Being swindled by Mansell was the greatest treat we children knew. We used to plead with him to give us his 'tests'. Only Jan and Chris and I were really old enough for them at this stage, but all of us clustered and clamoured around Uncle Mansell. The tests were riddles or puzzles and the fun lay not so much in working out the answers, although these were never too easy, but in getting Mansell to hand over the promised reward of a penny or twopence.

'Ah, but what I didn't tell you,' he'd grin, his dark brown eyes flicking from side to side with a look of cunning that I'm sure he cultivated, 'What I didn't tell you was that you've got to get at least two out of three', or: 'All right then, but let's make it fourpence if you can get this one as well'. 'Oh no!' we'd laugh and yell, jumping around with impatience. Twists and turns, excuses, doubling the odds, changing the rules, having no coins about him at the moment ... it was all up to expectation.

Mansell would reserve the quiz as a rare concession and sometimes it took half a day to pester him into it at all. He paid out maybe once or twice in a lifetime. I remember the solitary occasion on which he did so without evasion, 'A boat floating in a harbour has a line painted round it three feet above the water level. The tide comes in and the water in the harbour gets six feet deeper...'

It was Chris who spotted that the boat would rise with the tide and the line remain at the same level and who was handed the cash with a commendation for having applied his intelligence.

John, our youngest uncle, unmarried and still under thirty, also used to engage in tests with us, but it was we who asked him the questions. Jan and I usually had some tricky scientific problem waiting for him whenever he came over to Wolsey Road ('Why do you blow a candle to make it go out and blow a fire to make it burn up?'), for John possessed the largest fund of self-taught knowledge of anybody I have ever met. He had left school at fourteen but in the intervening years had probably studied more subjects more thoroughly than many a dedicated scholar. He filled Cambria with books. At this period he was living in Southend with Kitty and Mansell but always seemed to be in Hayes at weekends and often came over to Molesey. Having as yet no wife and children of his own, he was able to spend time with the three of us, being both a moral support for Mother and something of a father figure for Jan and me. Among the Jones brothers and sisters, he and Mother had always been closest.

To Jan and me, subjects such as the universe, the solar system and outer space, evolution, prehistory and the dinosaurs were of compelling fascination. Few books about such things were available for children and although we had *The Children's Encyclopaedia*, John was our living fount of knowledge – and not only broad sweeps of it but titbits of information. It was from him that we had first heard of a new type of pen, one with a tiny ball at the end instead of a nib,

78

and of a way to keep food fresh by freezing it. He seemed to have all the sciences at his fingertips as well as an easy command of literature, painting and music. Neither was the music merely theoretical, because the film of this story now unrolling before my mind's eye has a soundtrack and it includes John playing the clarinet, practising and practising for hours in one of the bedrooms at Cambria.

On the same soundtrack are the voices, all the Jones voices, animated in the ceaseless discussions with which the very walls of Cambria reverberated and which must be echoing around there still. Talk covered every imaginable topic – not only the arts and sciences, but religion, politics, psychology and current affairs, spiced with gossip and anecdotes about anyone we knew. Our Welsh blood was given the credit for the 'gift of the gab' on which we prided ourselves.

At a great gathering, lunch time would find us jammed shoulder to shoulder round the dining room table, and from there, as the meal ended, talkers and talk would drift, like the cigarette smoke that was everywhere, to the front room or the kitchen (the women did most, not all but most, of the cooking and clearing away), until at last with the dishes done and the tea made everybody could sit down again. All those who had married into the family learned to pitch into the ardent, serious and sometimes shouted interchange of opinions.

I used to love to sit and listen to it all, but the only one of the adults who stayed mainly quiet was Nan, and she was the one who became troubled when the men got into talks about 'the business' and passions grew heated over money. Then voices really rose and feelings could hardly be contained. The loudest argument I ever heard had Mansell, Ken and Gagga pacing the hall, too agitated to stay still, their faces scarlet, the veins standing out on Mansell's forehead. The sight was more than Nan could bear. 'You'll burst a blood vessel!' she cried, vainly trying to calm the angry males.

The 'business' was a family firm in which Gagga and all of them had some concern but which was chiefly run by Mansell. Its product was 'fancy goods'. This included musical jewel boxes and cigarette boxes of carved wood, with little rotating ballerinas popping up as the lids were opened and also goods made out of vellum – bookmarks, blotting pads, notepads and folders, all with hand-painted decoration done by Auntie Kitty, who was something of an artist. Down in Southend, Uncle Mansell had a workshop attached to his house where he employed about seventeen men and boys.

The business thrived, and Mansell was known to be the richest member of the family. He exulted in this image. Arriving at Cambria, he would stand there in the kitchen (everyone came in through the back door), a short, dark-haired man, urging you to feel the quality of his alpaca coat. 'Feel that, feel that, Val. What d'you think that cost? What d'you think? Nearly fifty quid! No kidding'. He proudly dressed Kitty in expensive clothes, too, with good jewellery and perfumes. She was no beauty but was slim, tall and elegant. Mansell would light up one of his fine cigars and speak of how the two of them had dined at some London nightclub, the Mirabelle or the Caprice, and of their planned holiday in the south of France. One was not always aware of the thread of melancholy running beneath the surface.

The display of tight-fistedness over handing out pennies for riddles was a game. In reality, Mansell was generous and responsible towards the rest of the family, helping where needed and once or twice paying for Christmas or a holiday for all.

* * * * *

Auntie Barb and Uncle Ken might have volunteered to be the ones to take Jan and me for the week that Mummy was in France, but no doubt we would have stayed there at some time during the year in any case, for we had been at least once before in the previous summers and would go again for years to come.

You would not imagine Guildford to be especially attractive as a holiday resort. It is not by the seaside. It is not one of the world's great cities – Venice, St Petersburg, Paris, New York. It is neither mountainous nor tropical, neither exotic nor

80

spectacular in any way. Jan and I stayed there with our uncle and aunt in a bungalow in Onslow Village, which is on the outskirts of the town, and our playmates were two children many years younger than ourselves.

Why is it then that our holidays there still fill me with such warm feelings of pleasure? I can only suggest a few reasons. One could have been that our expectations of a holiday, wherever it might be, were completely unsophisticated. Another might be that out of our own imaginations we produced such excitements and fantasies that only a small change of environment could transform our lives. And a third reason might be that we loved to return to familiar places. I, especially, already wallowed in nostalgia (note those recollections of 'the old summer evenings') and had built precious emotional structures out of past experience. We tapped into old associations evoked by the seasons, by music or by landscape.

The first time we went down there, Barbara had been worried about our being homesick. Despite our being so much older than her own children, Jan and I still seemed to her terribly young to be away from home. She was not to know that walks round the town or out on Grassy Hill, an occasional ride in the car with Uncle Ken, and a daily visit to the farm across the road were to become ritualised and repeated elements dear to our hearts. In addition, we found Vivien and Adrian highly entertaining, and now we had television there as well! Brumas the Bear (the baby polar bear born at London Zoo) was making his much publicised early appearances and Mystery Squadron, already mentioned, seems to have been tailor-made to fit in with that week of the holidays.

Auntie Barbara's meals were a novelty to us. She served many more salads than we would have tolerated at home but they were raised to a level of desirability almost on a par with fish and chips by the addition of one astounding ingredient: *cold* baked beans. And Ryvita! We devoured those biscuits as though they were obtainable nowhere in the world other than Guildford.

Altogether, in spite of poor weather, we were happily

occupied and were not homesick. The only problem seems to have been that I found it difficult to plait my hair by myself and one morning Auntie Barbara had to help me.

Uncle Ken, sometimes called Kandy, was in a way the quietest of my uncles and the one I now find hardest to describe. In boyhood, he had formed a contrast to Mansell, who, I've been told, tended to show the supposedly typical Napoleonic pugnaciousness of the short of stature, while Kenneth was tall and mild-natured, rather lacking in energy one would say. Certainly he was an introverted man, yet my picture memories of him include his regular Christmas party performance of Hey Winky Wum, and on our old cine films he can still be seen clowning around with Mansell. He probably needed the stimulus of others to bring out the livelier side of his character. I believe that to Ken more than any of the others the family was wholly sufficient. All the social contacts he required in this world were to be found among the Joneses and Barbara's people, and every individual who was added, by birth or by marriage, was incorporated into Ken's mental picture of his own group. Every now and then, the way he turned to you with a question or included you in the conversation, would reveal that this recognition applied as much to the children as to the adults. It felt as if he respected you.

Auntie Barb provided any energy that might be lacking in anyone else. She worked from morning till night, cleaning, cooking, sewing. I have seen her get out of the car with a needle in her hand, having carried on throughout the journey with the smocking of a little dress for Vivien. She could cycle across three counties, swim for hours at a stretch or walk all day long in the hills (and still can, I believe). She was wasted on such non sporty nieces as Jan and me, but we were used to lots of walking and I don't think we showed up too badly. With Vivien and Adrian being so small some activities would have been hampered anyway.

On 15th April Uncle Ken drove us back to Nan and Gag's, with Vivien coming along for the ride. *When we arrived Olwen had another boy, Julian Paul. Went to see it when it was 1½ hours old!* This was a thrilling experience. I took Vivien by the hand, telling her to be very, very quiet. We crept into Auntie Ollie's bedroom and gazed down at the sleeping baby, while Ollie herself lay smiling at us. I do not know why Jan was not there too.

Not for long was Julian an impersonal little 'it'. He came along just when I was at an age to be seriously capable of looking after small children and I probably wheeled him out in his pram more than any other of the young ones, with the result that a strong attachment formed between us and while he was a little boy we were each other's favourite cousins.

As for Auntie Ollie, for me she was – to use a late twentieth-century term that

Steven and Chris with Julian. 1951

would never have fallen from anyone's lips in 1950 – a role model, though neither of us knew it. Anything to do with weddings and babies was deeply attractive to me. The paraphernalia of bridesmaids, long dresses, prams, cots, shawls and matinée jackets fascinated me and would have done so even without any other influence, but Olwen happened to embody them. Hers had been the first wedding of my life; I had been her bridesmaid, aged two and a half. She had already by then given me my most important doll and thereby founded the doll family, some of which were named as the prototypes of the children I would have when I grew up (and I have the finished products to show for it).

83

It might sound as though Olwen were something of an 'earth mother' but she is really not at all the soft, lax, dreamy kind of person usually visualised in this connection. She is a strong person, shaped by hardship and by the struggle she and Yok had through those years to get by on an income smaller even than ours, with, eventually, four sons to bring up. Nor was she the only one of the adults around me to transmit the standards of family life that I took in: the pre-eminence of caring for children, the value above gold of a sound marriage. These were my mother's precepts too, though for her they had been marred. And so I was growing up to be one of the women of the family and when they were gathered in the lounge at Cambria with knitting and magazines – Nanny, Olwen, my mother and sometimes Barb and Kitty too – I would sit among them absorbing that rich peace which is created on such afternoons.

Women of the family: Barbara, Mother, Kitty 1951

* * * *

Unfortunately, by teatime on that day of Julian's birth I was sick, and I knew the cause. It was an excess of Ryvita and butter. Many children have made themselves sick on chocolates or rich party food but I managed to be sick from being greedy over Ryvita biscuits and had an aversion to them for many years afterwards.

I was well again by the next day.

Sunday April 16 Up one hour late. Forgot to put clocks on! Breakfast at 10.40, lunch at 3.0.p.m.! Did not see Julian today. Pity he's not a girl!

Went to Auntie Lizzie's to tea. Gagga took us but left us there for tea. They gave us silver bracelets. Very nice time. Gag fetched us home.

Over in Southall where Nan had grown up, where she and Gagga had been married and where all their five children had been born, there still lived a number of relatives from her branch of the family, the Syms. Closest to Nan were her two remaining sisters. One of her brothers, Uncle Jack, was still alive, but warm feelings on the part of other Symses towards his wife Gertie were somewhat lacking and also I understand that he tended to apply the religious principles of the Plymouth Brethren less sympathetically than the rest of them. So it was to Auntie Lizzie and Auntie Ettie, eldest and youngest of the original eight, our traditional pair of maiden aunts, that we went most regularly, to their terraced house in Kingston Road.

The two of them were of the same petite figure as Nan, five foot one or two, but without even the modest covering of flesh that she could boast. On their hands the webs of veins stood out in high relief and their faces were etched with the permanent creases of the fearfulness of life. The dark hair on each was parted and held back in a bun, never cut or styled as Nan's had been. Lizzie was hunch-backed and quite deaf, unaware of making a perpetual humming sound as she trotted busily back and forth.

At the sight of one of their great nieces or nephews the careworn faces would light up, the thin hands almost clap with

85

Family group in 1951

86

delight. We would be ushered in to find a filling spread at the tea table, for Lizzie baked her cakes with the confidence of one who had once worked her way through every domestic level from scullery maid to housekeeper in a large and wealthy household.

We knew the aunts to be poor but their generosity was almost as palpable as the tea pouring out of the pot. They handed us sixpences every time we saw them. On that day in April 1950, however, the scale of their giving exceeded anything that went before and as I look back on it now I realise that they gave us almost the most expensive presents of our entire childhood. I do not know the reason behind it, but a jeweller's tray was produced, in the Edwardian, upholstered formality of the front room, and we were invited to choose our favourites from a number of silver bracelets. It was not a difficult choice, I found, since among them was one of the most beautiful objects I had ever beheld (on which point my taste has not changed, in all the years, as I wear it still) and Jan decided upon the same but a narrower version of my design. A price of five pounds for each bracelet is floating in my memory. Did I see it attached on a tag or was it quoted openly to us? Is it likely that they cost so much? This is not clear.

* * * * *

Monday April 17   Breakfast in bed. Went out to play after I'd packed most of case and tidied room. Did some drawing.

Jan's going to start a club. 'Ivy Animal Club'. She spent a long time making plans. Chris has also started one. His is 'Eagle Club'. Held first meeting and, as Gagga was in a hurry, ate our tea at the same time.

Gag drove us home.

On this last morning at Nan and Gag's, while we are with Chris, although the activity we are involved in is not a game of cowboys, it seems the appropriate moment to introduce the history of the Gang. The Ivy Animal Club and the Eagle Club came to nothing but we cousins can still laugh over our crazy Gang after half a century.

87

It all started in the Christmas holiday of 1945 when Mother and Jan and I were staying with Auntie May in Torquay. Our holiday treats included a couple of visits to the Saturday morning pictures, and at least one of the films we saw was about Roy Rogers and his horse, Trigger. At the same time, among our Christmas presents were two popping guns, each consisting of a cone-shaped holder with a spring, controlled by a catch on the handle, from which to fire ping-pong balls. These toys instantly became our weapons and Jan and I became cowboys. Confined mainly to the house by wintry weather, we chased and raced and fired our ping-pong balls up and down the landing and all around and over Auntie May's four poster bed. She preferred us to play upstairs while the grown-ups had peace in the drawing room.

An invented character sprang into being – Bill Barno, the enemy, the 'baddy' that Jan and I were fighting.

As soon as we arrived at Nan's after Christmas (for this was one of the periods when we lived at Cambria for a few months, while Mother was getting the Wolsey Road flat made habitable) we brought Chris into the game and the Gang was formed. I was Roy Rogers himself, the Head of the Gang, but Jan and Chris and all future members had to choose their own names. Jan called herself Peter and she was the Second Head of the Gang. Chris became Jack and he was Third Head. Beyond us was a great band of imaginary followers and soon a whole elaborate world and way of life grew up.

Nothing could have been further removed from the lives of real cowboys or even from Western films. The Gang lived in Cowboyland in a splendid mansion called Mexico Camp House in which each man had his own well-furnished bedroom. Each man also had a wife or girlfriend and, of course, a horse. The horse had to be a palomino, like Roy Rogers's Trigger. We pronounced it 'palomino'. We designed uniforms, for ourselves as cowboys, for our prisoners, and for the women. The cowgirls' outfits drawn by Jan showed an uncanny foretelling of actual fashions of the future since they consisted of miniskirts worn with knee-high boots.

Any very young children who played with us, such as Steven,

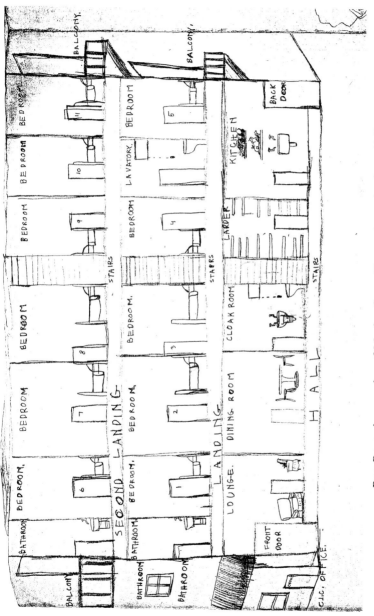

Roy Rogers's own plan of Mexico Camp House, drawn in about 1948

89

who was only a toddler at the beginning, and later in Wolsey Road the younger Fermor girls, were supposed to be members of the Training College. So was the imaginary son I decided Roy Rogers had to have, whose name, Vincent, linked my cowboy hero with that other hero of mine, Van Gogh. When one of the grown-ups, such as Nan or Gagga or our mother, happened to step on stage, as it were, by coming out of the back door to hang up the washing or fill the coal bucket, they were explained away as the 'servants' working at Mexico Camp House.

In April 1946 when we moved into the flat, Jan and I took the game with us. Chris retained his position as Third Head and resumed playing with us whenever we went over to Hayes but meanwhile we made friends with Paul Shepherd and initiated him as Fourth Head. When asked what name he would have, he thought for a moment and said 'Robber' and when informed that he had to have a girlfriend and must choose a name for her as well, he said without hesitation that she was called 'Darling'. Since Roy Roger's wife or girl was Peggy and Pete's was Val, Paul's choices certainly made the most original sounding pair.

Bill Barno reappeared from time to time, sometimes still as a villain but sometimes as one of us. The first of our cowboy songs was made up for Bill Barno, to a rather dirge-like tune:

> *We're glad Bill Barno's dead*
> *For he has wounded us,*
> *But now he's dead and gone*
> *And in his gra-ave thus.*

He never stayed dead for long. Neither did any of us. We had the Immortal Pills. At Wolsey Road we actually found a plant that served for this purpose. It was some tall flower which died off leaving a long woody stem within which was a dry spongy pith. It was easy to crack open the outer husk and take out lengths of the pith, breaking it into convenient pieces for its magical medicinal use. We never dreamed of really eating it, thank goodness, but we put it in our mouths without asking whether or not it were poisonous.

The song could be altered to '*We're sad Bill Barno's dead . . .*'

and so on if for that occasion he was on our side, and perhaps it was he who gave us the idea of converting all the baddies into goodies. We established a prison called Greenwood Camp. All our captives went into it and were given astonishing treatment. Members of the Gang waited on them hand and foot. We cooked them bacon and eggs. The crafty notion behind this was recruitment – to give them such a glowing picture of life in the Gang that they would plead to join us.

There was one reprobate among them, however, out of all those rival gangs and reformed German prisoners, one whom we could never trust: a character called Mister Derusky. In those days he gave us even more trouble than Bill Barno but now, fifty years on, it is his very name that is giving me trouble! How is it to be spelt? Whilst I am positive that the gentleman should always have his title MISTER, written out in full, as he was never referred to without it, I am not so sure what to do with 'Derusky' – Deruwski perhaps. At the time of his activities I never thought to see it set down in black and white, but the Polish flavour of such a name illustrates the hilarious hotch-potch of influences working on our minds immediately after the War.

Mister Derusky took a few beatings from us, and we were always very aggressive in the heat of battle. 'Pin 'em to the walls, boys' was our favourite cry as yet another phantom foe succumbed to our superior forces. Fortunately, our comfortable style of life in Mexico Camp House, which was set in vast grounds containing not only the Training College and Greenwood Camp but also a swimming pool, a private cinema and other luxuries, had not softened us.

There were other songs – marching songs, ballads and an anthem. The yearly anthem celebrated The Cowboy Emblem Leaves:

> *The Cowboy Emblem Leaves*
> *Wave in a gentle breeze.*
> *The sun shines down*
> *Upon the town,*
> *And the Golden Leaf he sees*

91

The leaf in question was the rowan and the song was composed one year when the rowans outside the gate at Cambria were in berry but why we didn't sing about the berry, so much more noticeable, I do not know.

We had a marching song, very brisk though a trifle over-emphatic in its message:

We are the cowboys, we are the cowboys, we are the cowboys marching along.
We are the cowboys, we are the cowboys, singing our famous cowboy song:
(then a change of key and tempo for the chorus):
We are the cowboys marching along,
Left, right, left, right, left, right, left, right,
Singing our famous cowboy song,
Left, right, left, right, halt!

The tunes were not too bad and I like to think the songs sounded less ridiculous than they now look on paper, especially considering our ages at the time of composition: myself nine or ten, Jan and Chris six or seven years old.

The greatest song of all recorded an event:

Roy Rogers was a cowboy,
And a merry gang had he,
He lived in Mexico Camp House
As happy as could be.

One night he woke and sniffed the smoke,
The flames all trembled near.
He said 'Mexico Camp House
Is on fire I greatly fear'.
   Chorus: Oh, Roy Rogers, (our only borrowed tune – *Oh Susannah!*)
   A merry gang had he ... and so on.

He looked out of the window
And he saw a fireman there,
But his pyjamas did come down
And he was nearly bare.
   Oh, Roy Rogers ... etc.

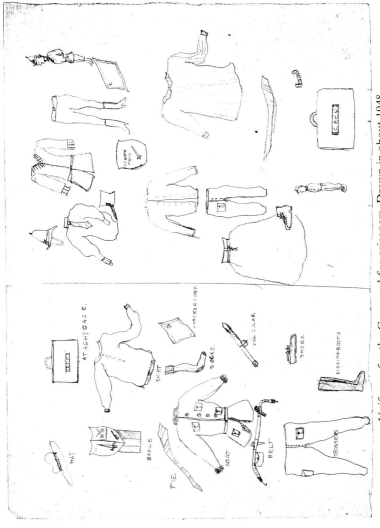

Uniforms for the Gang and for prisoners. Drawn in about 1948

93

Thank heavens I have forgotten all the other verses! Anyway, Mexico Camp House was burnt and had to be rebuilt and I think Bill Barno got the blame.

Whether at Cambria or Wolsey Road, we used the environment as a background landscape. The brussels sprout stalks in Gagga's vegetable garden were the original forest, Cambria Forest, where the first camp, according to our legend, had been built. In Paul's garden a small grassy rockery at one end of the lawn was a range of mountains. We could ride across them, rejoicing in the wind and ruggedness (they were about four feet high) and descend again to the plain. Or we could fortify ourselves behind the rocks and have gunfights with the enemy below. When the chase grew really wild we could run from the far end of Paul's garden across the open prairie, swerving clatter-footed up the narrow stone-paved passageway at the side of his house, with the danger of being ambushed, and then, if we got through, turn sharply into our own garden to dive through the stable.

We needed no props, not even toy guns. A piece of stick or two fingers of your own hand will always form a gun barrel.

The stories and ideas for most of our adventures would come pouring out of my head. I could lead the other children through a long, complicated drama lasting a whole morning or day, weaving the plot as we went along. The negative side of this was that I took my leadership very seriously – often far too seriously. Rules were strict. Not all the children who were subjected to its disciplines appreciated the importance of the Gang and the permanence of its formation. Those on the fringe who joined in with us only occasionally were not especially keen to be bossed around by me, and Jan now says that we were sometimes beastly to them!

The whole extraordinary institution endured for five years. It survived being transported between Hampton Court and Hayes and the changes of personnel which that entailed. I don't think the Third Head of the Gang ever met the Fourth Head or that there was any occasion when *all* the children who were supposed to belong to it got together. Neither do I think the game was ever played without both Jan and me. This would

have been the reason why I did not attempt to introduce it into
school playtimes, for the two of us could not have mixed in the
same group at school. Jan and Paul just possibly might have
played on their own now and then but I doubt it. If Jan and I
were alone we sometimes took on the roles of the wives, who
had a hierarchical structure reflecting that of their menfolk,
and their main occupation was to hold PT classes. The one
thing the Gang never did was herd cattle. We were not
bothered with the function of true cowboys.

The basis of our Gang games was obviously the age-old
theme of good versus bad and it is hardly surprising that this
should dominate the imaginations of wartime children, but we
played bad versus good as well. At various times, when not
playing cowboys, we acted bandits, gangsters and robbers and
there was a high degree of violence in much of our play.
Thursday April 6   Played all afternoon with Jan and Paul.

Cowboys, drawn by Jan, probably 1948 or '49

95

Richard was there a little while too. Made up a new game, Savages, involving torture, war dances and staining of arms and legs with sand. Our enemies were always imaginary. There was no rival real-life gang of children in Wolsey Road and when some of our number such as Jenny and Richard Bellears or the Fermor girls grew dissatisfied, they did not form up against the rest of us; they simply went off.

One day in November at school in an English lesson we were being cast for parts in plays. *I had to act a 'Slasher Knight', a bold heathen soldier,* I wrote. *Miss Duce said anyone less like a slasher knight than me it would be hard to find.* She might have changed her mind if she had seen me playing savages and bandits and charging round shooting people.

* * * *

Monday April 17 (continued)
Gag drove us home.
Good old Shoo had warm fire. We went to bed. Mummy came in at nine-thirty. How we leapt out, how we hugged her, how pleased we all were to be home. Auntie Kathline was with her. We were up till gone 10.30 with talking and giving gifts!
Tuesday April 18
Had so much to say! We've all enjoyed the holiday. All glad to be home! Mummy brought lots of gifts. Unfortunately Mummy starts college today.
I did some painting. Have done 6 pictures and some 'doodleing' and a card for Art holiday work.
Jan spent day at Zoo with Paul.
Got things ready for school tomorrow. Pam's invited me to Oklahoma on Saturday.

For Mummy the holiday had not been as wonderful as it sounds. She had been taken ill while sightseeing in Paris one day and Auntie Kathleen had had to hurry her back to the hotel in a taxi. And while not actually blaming a lack of cabbage for making her sick, she thought the French did not know how to cook vegetables properly. Poor Auntie Kathleen. For all her kind intentions, she could not understand that the

96

stimulation of travel which she found so refreshing did not have the same mental appeal for my mother and was physically wearing.

Our Easter break was rounded off by the fact that part of the dining room wall fell down on that last day.

4

SEX IN SUMMER

It was in our biology lesson on the first day of term that our
sex instruction began. The lessons were held in the Lecture
Room because the slide projector (the epidiascope) was needed
for illustration and the seats there were tiered so that everyone
could see the screen. Such teaching was new to the school and
we Lower Fourths were its first beneficiaries. We happened to
be at a critical time of life, twelve to thirteen years of age,
which in those days meant that half of us already knew the
facts of life, half did not, and most of us probably knew
something but not everything.

It was also new to the nation as a whole and heated
arguments had been published in the press for and against the
idea that children should be given such lessons in school. For
this reason, LEH had had to take the precaution of writing to
our parents about it and asking for their consent.

A brief part of the first lesson was spent on a sort of 'birds
and bees' introduction, but the film strips came round pretty
quickly to the main topic: human reproduction. The birds and
bees (or fishes and plants, I think, to be exact – bees came later
as a subject in their own right) were in fact brought in for
comparison between them and us in the matter of fertilisation.
We were shown the two types of fertilisation, external and
internal, and it was internal fertilisation that brought us
straight to the nub of things. There on our screen was a
diagram of a penis inserted into a vagina.

They both appeared to have been drawn with a ruler, giving
no indication of the actual physiology of intercourse other
than through the use of the words 'erection' and 'ejaculation',

and little sign of the human bodies that the organs belonged to.

I was one of those to whom this part of the process of having babies was new. At home that evening I talked to Mummy about what I had learned and asked her how people could sometimes have an 'accidental baby'. Her explanation was that when people are in love they sort of *want* to do it – like kissing. So this was *the* crucial Fact of Life. I recognised it instantly as something important and true, a piece of knowledge for which my mind had been waiting. Whatever I had previously thought was meant by 'mating' with reference to the newts in the pond, I do not remember, but I do know that the days when I could be innocently puzzled by the actions of two pigeons 'who seem to be acting a circus ... one climbed on the other's back just now' – were over.

Mother's policy of transmitting information of this kind to her children had been to answer questions honestly when they were asked. The trouble with this is that children do not always think of the most useful questions to ask. It does not necessarily occur to them to follow logically from knowing that a baby grows in its mother's 'tummy' to wondering how it got there in the first place. There would have come a day, I suppose, when Mother would have had to sit me down and pass on any unsought but vital bits of knowledge; although, on second thoughts, she would have found some subtle means of bringing me round to asking the questions. Luckily, Miss Cooke's film strip had had this same effect.

I wonder what Miss Cooke's feelings were on having to handle this experimental and potentially difficult lesson. She was a small, neat, quietly spoken woman, out of school a devout Baptist and a leader of the chapel youth group, the Covenanters. Except for her maidenly status, she seemed ideally suited to the task, delivering the commentary to accompany the slides with clinical calmness. As a science teacher, she wore a white coat for most of her lessons and, despite the quietness, she did not lack authority. She was the senior biology mistress. I imagine, though, that she might have had qualms beforehand about possible fits of giggles and silliness among the class as she stood there pronouncing words that perhaps she had never uttered out loud in her life before.

Showing us the slides occupied three lessons. They soon progressed to what was, in fact, their main subject, namely the development of a baby in the womb. It was this that was regarded as the great fascination and a marvel of nature and this which was almost certainly new to every girl, for how many parents in those days, let alone children, would have ever seen such pictures? But it was this also which led to giggling and whispering talks in the playground. Silliness over sex erupted in a way it had never done before. It was quite definitely brought about by our sex education lessons and would not have happened without them, but it all took place outside them. It reflected the emphasis of the lessons, which had been not upon sex as such but upon babies. It was the notion of having a baby inside one's tummy that became a source of innuendo and dirty jokes, for it was as if smuttiness was an instinct like any other, or a facet of the sex instinct as a whole, and had to be expressed in whatever form came to hand. It may also have been that the startling new knowledge caused all kinds of adolescent forces to come bursting out; or it may have been a way of dealing with embarrassment.

The irony of it was that the whole movement towards openness in sexual knowledge was intended to banish smuttiness. The generation that had grown up in the 1920s and 1930s scorned Victorian prudery. When asked for their consent to our sex lessons, none of our parents refused and rare indeed would have been the mother or father in the 1950s set upon keeping a daughter in ignorance about sex. They believed in ending ignorance, in sexual truthfulness for children, in a clean, healthy, open attitude. They believed in the ideal which proclaimed that sex was a fine, natural, wonderful thing, that love between man and woman and the bearing of children the greatest experiences in life and that, given this attitude, pornography, dirty jokes and embarrassment would become redundant and fade away. No one would have a need for them.

Even the disputes in the press over the teaching of the facts

100

of life were not so much to do with whether children should be taught them or not but to do with who should teach them – families or schools.

Against all this, it was the daughters who were reactionary, not the parents. We were still shy. We still cringed inwardly at having to read aloud in class any passage from Shakespeare containing the word 'breast' and were thankful that a verse of a hymn might be omitted if it would have meant singing the line 'offspring of the Virgin's womb'. We did not want to be open and frank.

Some of our mentors were more determined than others to sweep away old inhibitions and to knock out of us girls all undesirable coyness. One of these was Miss Griffith who took over from Miss Miller as our PT teacher later in the year. If one of us sidled up to her in the changing room and whispered a request to be let off games, Miss G. would reply in a loud voice for all to hear: 'Trouble with your monthly periods, eh?' The rest of us would pretend not to hear, all feeling embarrassment on our classmate's behalf.

My mother was of the same school of thought as Miss Griffith. Like so many others, she was very much influenced by her own childhood when a question such as 'What does "womb" mean?' would receive the response, 'It's something in the Bible,' and when a girl could be completely unprepared for menstruation. She was strongly determined to see euphemisms and evasions banished and I shocked her very much on one occasion when I told her there were girls of my age who still used that antiquated term 'the curse'. 'That would have been considered terribly out of date when I was young!' she exclaimed.

The obverse side of the mission towards sexual enlightenment, however, was that humour was dropped along with the prudery and the porn, so that no one ever spoke lightly, say, of parts of the body or their functions. This was particularly true of the Jones family, with its very earnest, serious, Welsh inheritance. Everything had to be factual, proper and rather solemn. Only correct anatomical words were used and as a result I managed to reach well into adulthood without being fully

101

acquainted with: crap, shit, turd, tits, arse, prick, cock, balls (except in their un-debased meanings) and many, many others.

It was possible, then, to grow up in a different kind of ignorance. Family and school combined, unintentionally, to give a 'sheltered' background. A most striking illustration of this was the almost total absence of swearing. Social standards demanded that men refrained from using bad language in the presence of women and a man would apologise if the odd expletive slipped out. But with us, the men of the family (except John) never swore in any company. The unspoken proscription sprang from Gagga, for beneath his roof any utterances that took the name of God in vain or bore the slightest disrespect for religion were unthinkable. Thus one would never even say 'My God!' or 'Good Lord!' and as for 'Jesus Christ' or 'Bloody Hell!' they would have been more terrible than words can describe.

I took it for granted that the majority of swear words had a religious connection, for I knew that bloody referred to the blood of Christ and any that, as far as I could tell, did not, like bugger, had come into use simply because they sounded forceful. They began with B and contained other hard consonants. The only cry of anger that might pass Gagga's lips was 'Bother!' which confirmed these observations. It confirmed too that there was a scale of depravity, rising (or descending) from the harmless Bother to the worst B word of all – Bleeding.

This neat theory of B words was temporarily shaken, however, one day a few months after Miss Cooke's sex classes. Standing in a line in our form room, waiting to file out to a lesson elsewhere, I overheard a girl further along say a word beginning with F. My nearest companion in the line, Janet Barrell, whispered to me 'That is the worst swear word there is!' I was very puzzled. 'Are you sure?' I queried, but she nodded emphatically. We moved on at that point and there was never any more discussion of it, but I decided afterwards that Janet must have been mistaken. How could such a soft, ineffective little word be a swear word?

* * * * *

102

Saturday April 22   Went to Pam's in p.m. In evening went to
Oklahoma. Wonderful! Fine show. Bed at 11.p.m.
  Sunday April 23   Woke late. Made a house with bed clothes
and had breakfast in it. Were not up till gone 12.30! Had lunch
there (Pamela's house). *Played till tea time. Came home at*
7.0p.m. Has been a good weekend.

Pamela was thirteen on the 21st April and *Oklahoma* was her
birthday treat. All of us loved it, her parents, Pamela and I and
another, older girl, Bridget, a friend of Pamela's from when she
had lived in Wraysbury, who came with us. I had never been
taken to a musical before and on the Sunday I went home in
raptures. It was one of the most marvellous things I had ever
seen.

'I'm going to save up and take you to see it for your
bithday!' I declared to Mummy, but to my surprise she hastily
put me off. 'No, it isn't the sort of thing I would want to go
to', she said and then I discovered that, just as with the books
we read, there were criteria to be observed. There was
something slightly inferior about musical comedy; it was not
serious theatre and on at least one later occasion I heard
Mother or Uncle John speak derisively of the genre. As I grew
older I gradually realised that a thick streak of intellectual
snobbery coiled through our family.

It was partly due, I assume, to the Joneses' perception of
having nothing to get on in the world with except their intelligence and to the justifiable belief that their intelligence was
above the average. Mother's generation was the first to have
had any really worthwhile chance at a good education, through
winning places for themselves at grammar schools, but it was
their sons and daughters who were meant to go even further.
We were to set our sights high and to cultivate our minds to a
superior level.

I hope I shall be forgiven for being proud of my family, as I
was, and even for the brashness of regarding them as being
almost a special sort of dynasty, not of the common herd. But
I think that from that night of having seen *Oklahoma*
something in me was set against the narrow outlook that could
not enjoy musicals and that turned away from sheer light-

hearted fun. Anyway, the narrowness did not last. I am happy to say that Mother in the end let herself be unreservedly lured by such pleasures as *South Pacific*, *Seven Brides for Seven Brothers* and *Guys and Dolls*.

Much of the fun that I did have as a girl was due to Pamela and her parents. I visited them far more often than Pamela visited us, for I could spend the night there, while except for that one emergency in the smog we could not offer similar hospitality. Mother was desperately conscious of the inadequacies of the flat compared with the comfort of Pamela's home and she certainly thought it impossible for herself to be on equal social terms with anyone like Mr and Mrs Fish – not because they were grand or aloof in any way, for they were extremely kind people, but because, being on her own and with the restrictions imposed by lack of money and by studying, she could never have reciprocated an invitation. She could not have entertained them to dinner nor taken them out for an evening.

There were friends, however, whom we visited or who did come to the flat to see us. Mother's fellow students from college sometimes dropped in and one evening after the college year had ended *Mummy's friends came to supper. Daphne and Dick and others.* They must have eaten in the kitchen because Jan and I *went to bed while they had a nice time!* There were many evenings in 1950 when the Diary says, 'Mummy was out late', and though this must often have been due to college functions or working late, I am sure she had a circle of friends and a rich social life at Hampton.

The closest friends we had as a family were Joan and Peter Green. In 1950 Joan and Peter were still quite newly married and lived with Joan's mother, Mrs Pern, in West Molesey. It was through Uncle John that we knew them, and it was because of their like-minded love of books and discussions that they became more or less honorary members of the family. We regarded them as connoisseurs of all that was new and stylish and, once they had moved into a house of their own, their furniture and fabrics and decor were of keen interest to the three of us throughout this period. It was Joan and Peter who

104

Joan and Peter

introduced us to the fashion of painting one wall of a room in a different colour from the rest. It was Joan and Peter who fitted kitchen shelves made of a wonderful new material called Formica. It was Joan and Peter who had a dinner service with each setting in a different, vibrant colour. All very 1950s! They often called on us on a Saturday afternoon when they had been shopping, or when they knew John was coming over, and we in turn would be invited to tea with them.

Saturday June 17 Went to Joan and Peter's to tea. Girl called Christine (Joan's niece I think) was there. We played in Joan's garden. Stripped their cherrie trees almost bare. Strawberries for tea. Peter played with us a bit. He drove us home in car with Christine.

Sunday December 17 Went to Joan and Peter's in P.M. Had a wonderful tea. Then they showed us their dancing clown, their toy theatre, and Mrs Pern dressed up as Father Xmas. Home late. We wished them a Happy Christmas.

The one other family friend seen most frequently during the year was Miss Simpson.

Ruth Simpson was the gifted child psychiatrist who had treated me in Scarborough during the War for the nervous disorders I suffered as a result of our broken home and the bombing. It was Miss Simpson who has already been mentioned (in Chapter 2) as having helped Mother as well as

105

me in that low period of her life by engaging her on a voluntary basis to visit and deal with some of the problem families encountered in the course of psychiatric work. Most important of all, she was the link between ourselves and Auntie Kathleen, and it was through her therefore that we had come to the flat. I imagine it would have seemed a perfect formula for restoration on both sides to bring together an old friend who had lost a daughter and a new friend with two daughters who needed a home and a peaceful place to begin anew.

Ruth Simpson

Miss Simpson too had come back down south from Scarborough at the end of the War and her centre, or 'The Playroom' as children always called it, was now at Epsom. We saw her on several occasions in 1950 when she came to Wolsey Road to stay with Auntie Kathleen, but sometimes, for a treat rather than treatment, we still loved to visit the Playroom. *Thursday November 9 Half-term, hurray! Jan and I cleared up room when Mummy had gone. About 10.0, in our best clothes and with lunch packed in bag, we set off for Miss Simpson's. Long bus ride to Epsom. Miss Simpson met us with her cousin Olive, and a corgi dog, Merry, in a car. Started right away when we got to the playroom. I made some clay models – a Santa Claus and a funny old man. With a lot of Miss Simpson's friends we had a picnic lunch. I painted my models. Jan made a jungle and a farm in a sand-tray. We wanted to buy some clay to take home but it was too expensive.*

(To digress briefly as a point of interest: the sand trays were used by Ruth Simpson to form an especially important part of her assessment of a child. They were like large, shallow boxes three or four feet square, on short legs, holding a few inches of sand. With dozens of model buildings, trees, people, vehicles and animals to choose from, you could make a 'world' in your sand tray. Miss Simpson told me when I was older that my early worlds had been grim, fenced-in places but that later on I had produced pleasant country landscapes. The emotional interpretations are obvious.)

Apart from these sociable comings and goings, we did not lack for other outings and entertainments. Early in the year I tagged along to see the ballet at Sadlers Wells with a group from the Rectory Modern School, where Mother was doing her school practice: *First time I've seen ballet. Valses Nobles et Sentimentiles, Sea Change, Beauty and the Beast, Kingdom of Sweets. Beautiful show.* In June, we joined a coach load of students from Hampton College on a coach excursion to St Albans, and in July at the college itself we saw some of those same students perform *The Bartered Bride.* The Royal Academy Summer Exhibition made another 'first' for me. *It's fun having Mummy home! She and I went to London today. We went by train. Looked over Royal Academy. Couldn't do it all, of course, but we saw most of the work. Some was jolly good, some not so well done. Two of Mr Keefe's were there. They were good.* Arnold Keefe was the art tutor at Hampton who had become friendly with Mother.

Then there were our own school outings, to Haselmere for instance in May: *Started from home at 8.45 a.m. Poor Pamela felt sick on the way in the coach. Looked all round museum before lunch. Nice man showed us things. Took picnic lunch in grounds. Explored grounds. Microprojector show. Picnic tea at Hindhead on way back.* As far as I can remember we were meant to have the picnic tea in the Devil's Punchbowl but it was too wet. It was wet also on the day we went to Regent's Park: *Long train journey with everyone to Open Air Theatre. Merchant of Venice was very good. It rained though and we all went into a big tent to watch it.*

From time to time there would be a school friend's birthday

party, Susan Braybrook's in the Christmas holiday having already been described, with another on 4th March: *Bridget Wolf's birthday. She had six of us to tea. Smashing food. Nice time.*

One Saturday in January we three went dutifully together to a party given by our 'old retainer', Rose Keach. Rose was Shoo's predecessor. It may seem remarkable now that even when hard up and living in a four-roomed flat, Mother employed a charlady even if for only one day a week. But cleaning, washing and ironing were far harder then and far more women were willing to do domestic work for a few shillings. Rose lived in Feltham with her elderly mother. *Rose's party in afternoon. Not looking forward to it but it turned out very good ... Rose has a sweet mother, very tiny house. Lots of people came. Grand fun.* This was a typical example of our Appleby reluctance to be sociable. We were afraid of having to join in the games, to act like extroverts and make fools of ourselves. We nearly always had a good time in the end.

Some while after this, Rose, who was in her fifties, was wooed by a widower and her

Mrs Keach and Rose

wedding reception was similar to the earlier party. I remember how guests squeezed round the table in two shifts, how the sink got blocked with tea leaves, and how a fat, friendly woman organised us all in a spirit of knees-up jollity and joked about double beds, while Rose in her blue silk dress smiled

108

with true bridal nervousness, and the stepdaughter glowered at this new mother.

When it came to entertainment, it is surprising that we did not make more use of Molesey's small cinema, the Court, that lay no more than a hundred yards from our door, but we seem to have gone only twice in 1950. The first was in August one day when Mummy was out.

Shoo, Jan and I had salad together. We got washed up quickly. Pictures! Paul came round and joined us but got his own money. We went to the 'Court'. First film not so nice. About battle of El Alamein in last war. News and trailers, then (super!) 'Happiest Days of Your Life!'

The second time was in the Christmas holiday. *Went to Pictures over road with Shoo. Saw not such a nice film with Jean Simmons getting two husbands or some nonsense.*

Mummy took me once more to the ballet towards the end of the year, the Ballet Rambert, I believe, in Kingston. I can only presume that Jan was offered the chance to come with us and rejected it – or was she considered still too young to sit through a whole afternoon of the finer performing arts?

* * * * *

Thursday April 20   Summer time! School has that good old Summer Term feeling.

Just for a brief spell, it did. Curtains were put up in the form rooms, the pale yellow cotton curtains that came out every year and blew in the warm breeze from the open windows while softening the sunlight into a luminous glow across our desks and creating an idyllic picture to take into the future – at least, that was how it was meant to be. As if to urge the season forward with an act of faith, I shed my grey overcoat for a blazer, but it was still only April and the elements saw this not as faith but *hubris,* for *Oh day of days, it SNOWED!* A frozen week followed during which the lilac was weighed down and broken, we spent lunch hours indoors and I developed the almost inevitable feverish sore throat.

Summer will be altogether dreary, say experts. I feel worse than the weather! I recorded, yet we persisted in hope, sewing name tapes into the summer dresses for which we had been measured at school by the lady from Peter Jones back in the winter, and not even waiting for May to be out before wearing them. The pinnacle of optimism was reached in early June when we wore summer vests for the first time! Then indeed we were rewarded with a hot spell and when I was sweating over my prep in the garden that evening, Colonel Gettins came out with choc ices. *Bless him!* I wrote somewhat condescendingly.

The uniform summer dresses came in a choice of three colour schemes – red and white stripes, green and white stripes or blue and white stripes – and would have imparted a giddy sense of freedom from our serviceable winter grey had they been slightly more stylish. At least one could say that their full gathers both in the bodice and the skirt could accommodate any size or shape of girl, and they were cool. At one time Panama hats had been a mandatory part of the summer uniform but by 1950 a red or grey beret was allowed at any time of the year. One needed to possess a velour hat, however, for outings and public occasions.

Jan and I each had one dress of each colour. I think we kept to the same rotation system as we did with our white blouses, with Mondays and Thursdays being clean dress days. I don't know whether Jan ever had any new dresses of her own or whether my old ones were kept for three years to be handed down to her.

* * * * *

There was nothing hand-me-down about the First of May. It was Jan's birthday and she was the May Queen. In other years, when it had not fallen on a school day, we had done the thing properly with a procession and a crowning, bringing all our local friends into it. It was a romantic and attractive date to have been born on and luckily no suggestion ever reached us that its ancient rituals with ribbons and maypoles could be debased into some heavy-footed 'Labour Day'.

110

In 1950 when it fell on a Monday and only Paul shared it with us, I spent most of the weekend beforehand wrapping gifts, making candles and icing biscuits for the birthday tea. We managed to expand the cornucopia of gifts by providing little parcels in the names of toys and animals.

Jan's birthday. 10 years old. I was awake at six, Jan woke at 6.30. Opened gifts straight away. She had a toy cat from Mr P. Esqu., chocs from Teddy and co., recipe book from Mummy, record from me, sixpence from each cat. Teddy danced all over bed.

By the time we came home for tea, Shoo would be waiting with her present and the post would have brought cards, usually containing postal orders, from Nanny and Gagga, from most of the aunts and uncles and from our father. Some of the cash would almost immediately be turned around and posted back to Hayes, for Chris's tenth birthday was only eight days later, and *we sent him 3/6 postal order and 2/6 for Baby Julian.* The apparently rather mean little gift from Mummy was not a symptom of our poverty but a stopgap pending the collection of the main present, which Mummy brought home a couple of days later: a Pelham puppet. *Last night Mummy bought Jan two string puppets. One was a gift, one Jan had bought with birthday money. A dog and an ostrich. They are cute and we now can make them look quite real. Jan lets me work them sometimes.* Pelham puppets were classic and beautifully made toys but they demanded some skill if one were to avoid hopelessly tangling up their strings.

Despite an age difference between us amounting to twenty five per cent at this stage, Jan and I were constant companions and exceedingly important to one another. I recall that we also had many violent fights, but according to the Diary this is a false memory, unless for some reason 1950 was an exceptionally harmonious year. There does not seem to have been one single quarrel. Our two personalities have always been judged by others to be as chalk and cheese, with Jan perceived as the rebel, uncooperative (at school, anyway), the tougher one and more hot tempered. From the very beginning it was only too easy to take one look at her copper-coloured hair and label her 'redhead', with all the attributes that that is supposed to carry.

111

I was seen as docile and reserved, 'highly strung' but easier to deal with so long as not emotionally upset. Needless to say, our package of chromosomes is not really divided like the butter ration as neatly as these ready résumés imply.

In 1950 we were still two little girls together, but it would not be for much longer. Not only would the age gap grow into a 'maturity gap' as I reached the mid-teens, but Jan would branch off into an interest and a group of friends that I never joined. She became horsy and her great love of animals formed the framework of her life for many years. Meanwhile, we painted and wrote stories, we played cowboys and we played with dolls.

Monday September 4 Jan and I went into garden early and stayed out. Lovely weather. We played cowboys, then cleaned Rose Cottage and brought five dolls out. Jan and I were two women (my husband killed, hers fighting) who had been bombed and now lived in a one-roomed shack with our children. Were poverty-stricken, couldn't afford to send children to school! Worked to make clothes for them and grew most of our own food.

This deliciously tragic drama was a variation on our traditional theme of 'ladies' but we no longer always played on such an equal footing. The Diary references show that I made clothes or wrote tiny books 'for Jan's dolls', 'made a fireplace for Jan of card', 'made more toys for Jan' or 'we built a miniature garden'. The pleasure now for me was evidently more in the attendant craft work than in the game of dolls.

Was it that I clung to Jan for want of other company? As if it were decreed by fate, I was always an eldest child – eldest one in the family, eldest among our neighbours wherever we happened to live and at school almost the oldest in my year. One might ask, what would I have done with myself if I had scorned to play with younger children? I know, however, that this was not the reason that I stayed close to Jan. There were alternatives, after all: solitude for one, which I had never minded, and for another, girls such as Tina nearer to my own age in Wolsey Road whom I could have joined. No, I was close to Jan by choice. Even one weekend of separation from her, when I was going to Nan's while she remained at home, held no attractions, for I wrote that I wished she were coming with me. We tended to be exclusive. We included other children reluctantly unless we knew them well and even Paul had had to break through a pretty frosty barrier to become our friend.

At school I seem to have taken on a protective attitude towards Jan. Perhaps watchful is a more accurate word, since she hardly needed protection, but she was still only in her first year at LEH and I think I wanted to know that she was all right. In addition, it pleased me to show her off. Some siblings hardly impinge on one another. With us, even a minor encounter was apparently worth noting in the Diary; I wrote things like: *Met Jan coming over for lunch* or *Saw Jan in break*. I recorded her achievements...

January 11 Jan is vice form captain in her form.

March 6 Jan's acting Harriet in 'Harriet and the Matches'. She's excellent. Best actress in her form.

September 26 Jan came home and announced she's got an Art Prize! 10/- to spend. We were all so pleased.

... and her failings: *I saw Jan going* [to the prizegiving]. *Her hair was <u>awful</u> of course, as it always is on important occasions.*

Strangely enough, there were fewer girls than you might expect who could boast a similar acquisition: a sister lower down the school. I wanted everyone to see her as a clever and unusual person. Jan's own angle on it was rather different though, I suspect, at any rate as betrayed by one particular incident: *June 2 Had lunch early with Juniors. Saw Jan, who kept running over (provided teacher's back was turned) and blowing kisses at me.* Surely this was mockery, not affection, an age-old, irresistible teasing and a ganging up of her group, like a bunch of young chimps darting and poking at their seniors.

One possible area of trouble between us would have been the Diary. The Diary was kept, apparently, in 'my top drawer' with 'all my little private treasures' in a chest. The drawer certainly had no lock and the typical script here would have had Jan sneaking a look, my discovering she had done so and the climax a furious row. There is not even a faint echo in my memory of anything like this happening. Perhaps she did peek

113

and I never found out. As for Mummy, I don't think I would have feared for a moment that she would look in my Diary.

Mummy always swore that she had no favourite. There was not an ounce of difference in her love for each of us and she tried to treat us with scrupulous equality. Among friends and relations, I had the advantage of having been well established in their affections long before Jan was born and was, for example, Gagga's favourite, but there were always those who found Jan the more attractive child and one of them was Shoo. Shoo and Jan had in common their love of animals, particularly horses (although it was on the racetrack I think that Shoo loved them best), and where Mummy would take me to the ballet, Shoo would take Jan to some event of mutual interest to the two of them. During the weekend mentioned above, for instance, *Jan has had a nice time while Mummy and I were at Nan's. She went with Shoo to Ottershaw woods, horse show and fair.*

Shortly after this, one Saturday in June, *Shoo walked in with a tortoise for Jan!* This was not just an act of kindness but something vital to Jan's life. Wise Shoo! Jan *needed* an animal. Loving dogs and horses in the abstract was not enough. Having the Gettins' cats in the house was not enough and neither were our tropical fish, for Jan had to have a creature of her own to care for, one that was capable of responding to and loving her in return. It was a dog, of course, that she longed for. Yet how could we keep a dog in the flat? It seemed out of the question; and then, about three years later, another percep- tive and sympathetic observer with Jan's interests at heart persuaded Mummy to reconsider the idea. This person was Ruby Davies, Jan's form mistress at the time, and her sugges- tion carried such weight that Mummy discussed it with the Gettins. The outcome was that Auntie Kathleen and the Colonel magnanimously agreed to have a dog in their house and in their garden. In the meantime, however, with Jan still only ten, the less demanding Timothy Tortoise filled the bill. It was the first pet wholly her own and he did not want for devoted attention. He was taken to school several times and used as a model in the art room. Shoo's instinct had accurately picked up the need.

114

Not that our lives had been devoid of animal company before. The cats upstairs have already been mentioned. They were Sandy, a large Orlando-like chap with what we called a 'rumptious' purr and an incurable habit of flexing his claws on your knees when he sat in your lap, and Auntie Kathleen's beloved old Ali Shan. Ali Shan never came down to our flat. We would see him mainly in the garden. He was a one-woman cat. On summer days, Auntie Kathleen, having tea outside, would 'ring' for him with a teaspoon on her saucer and his elderly grey figure would pace in a dignified manner across the lawn to be given a drink of milk. One day in October 1950 Ali Shan was found dead at the roadside, run over, a few streets away in Molesey. *Auntie K. very upset ... we are all sad. I cried. He was nearly 17, been with her since a tiny kitten.* The next day she buried him beside the bay tree in the garden and planted two rosemary bushes, 'rosemary for remembrance', on his grave.

But Auntie Kathleen could not be without a cat, and before the end of the year she had acquired his successor whom she named Barnabas because, she explained, it meant 'Son of consolation'.

At some time during the summer of that year, we three had taken in a little stray which we called Sootsy, but I don't think she stayed for more than a few months. In the Diary I accused Shoo of spoiling her by feeding her fish at irregular times. Then for a couple of weeks in the summer, yet a further specimen of *Felis catus* was added to the ménage. This was Beau who was of the same refined, grey-blue breed as Ali Shan and who belonged to Auntie Kathleen's son, Denis. We were also visited by Mitsy, a silky, long-haired pedigree cat who used to come over the wall from number 5 to play with us. She belonged to Mrs Bowling, wife of our doctor, and both cat and mistress exuded to an uncanny degree the same air of charm and elegance. Poor Beau was rather timid, apparently, and came off badly in an encounter with Mitsy: *Beau, Dennis's cat, is staying here while they are away. Mitsy came to play ... At teatime, Dennis introduced Beau to her. Spitfire Mitsy went for him!*

115

There was only one dog in the vicinity and he was our neighbour on the other side, Stumpy, the little West Highland White terrier that ran at the heels of Paul's father, Walter Shepherd. Cats were the thing in Wolsey Road. Beyond the Shepherds, at number 11, Mrs Littlejohn had thirteen of them, but they kept themselves to themselves.

A postscript on the subject of tortoises: *Saturday June 24 Paul's home for his half term.* [He was now at boarding school.] *I went to play. As soon as he saw Jan's tortoise he wanted one. He got a smaller one. We had a christening in somerhouse. Its name is Buddy. Unfortunately he lost it about an hour later. They're still hunting now.* And it appears that Buddy had gone for good.

* * * * *

For school children, teachers are a never-ending source of interest, and the Diary contains numerous comments on the ones at LEHS:

Thursday March 16 In P.S. Miss Firth got a bit wild because everyone dropped books, etc., and she said 'Don't expect one of you will ever be in the sixth form'.

Thursday April 20 Miss Firth not in very good mood in P.S. Trouble with her is she can't help laughing at silly things we say. Also she goes back on her word and doesn't give punishments that she promises.

Thursday June 1 I've a good mind to complain about Miss Firth. She called us GUTTERSNIPES last lesson! She's a fool 'cause she gives people detentions and then takes back the slips. She can't keep order. She's rude.

Miss Firth was our unluckiest victim. Once a week she had to sit with us through a private study period. The fact that it was not a formal lesson but a time for doing our prep was part of the reason why we did not take it seriously, but there is no question that if Miss Denney, say, had been supervising we would have got on with our work. Miss Firth simply could not keep order. She had been in the school only since January, so we must have marked her as our prey immediately. At our first

116

encounter with her we must have detected some flaw in her authority and we exploited it mercilessly ever after. Clearly she made a fool of herself by flinging out too many punishments in the first place, but the poor woman was probably at her wits' end.

Another who came close to this loss of control on occasion, but as an exception to the general conduct of her lessons, was Miss Hepburn who taught French. *Miss Hepburn told Pat J. to go to Miss Lacey* [deputy headmistress] *but I think she's afraid Pat would hit her or something. Pat made an excuse and Heby let her sit down. That's often happened before.*

Once or twice, by simply grumbling about some task, we were let off doing it, and all these incidents go to show that discipline was not as smooth in the past as is sometimes believed. We were well brought up girls enjoying a private education in the days when, it is often fondly thought, the young respected their elders and did not dare defy them, yet we were obviously quite unruly.

Miss Denney, history mistress, stood at the other end of the spectrum from Miss Firth. Except for a year or two of her early career she had been with LEHS all her life, as pupil and teacher. She had come through two world wars with the school and was once heard to say that if another broke out she did not know how she would bear it. I cannot define the essence of her authority, but there she would stand, hands folded in front of her, sometimes gazing into the distance as she talked, as if seeing like a mirage out on the playing field the Spanish Armada or a feudal village or Parliament repealing the Corn Laws, and never needing to threaten anyone with a random detention. *History with Miss Denney is super!* was my verdict, *She just keeps you enthralled. She goes into all sorts of different discussions but seems to get on quite quickly…*

It wasn't always the staff with a significant part to play in my school life who came in for the most attention in the Diary. About Miss Sturrock, the art mistress, for example, I had little to say because in art my position was secure, there was no interesting friction or resentment to report and I would never have dreamed of making fun of her. I happily produced stacks of extra paintings completed in the holidays, loved learning a new skill such as italic lettering or lino printing, and was sometimes more critical of my own work than she was. Conversely, Miss Patterson, who taught needlework, was the subject of a see-sawing commentary with a fresh episode nearly every week. A selection of entries reads:

Had needlework this afternoon. Patty in excellent mood. She started an interesting discussion on clothes.

Patty in a paddy! She made us stop work half the afternoon. Can't see what good it does us. Only put us behind. She promised to give us a detention but didn't.

I'm getting on with tray cloth in needlework. Patty asked some of us what we did in hols. at end of lesson. I like her for taking that interest in us.

Patty gave us a long lecture about selfishness. We did some needlework revision.

Miss Patterson is so funny, poor soul! She looks at you with her chins doubling and undoubling, her hands screwing up. We came out in fits of laughter.

I wonder if the time spent on this acute observation of Miss Patterson would have been better directed at my needle and thread and improving the quality of my slow, rather messy work.

Our mirth was not always of the cruel, mocking kind. There were times when we laughed with, not at, our teachers:

Miss Hodge for Latin. [In place of our usual teacher] *She kept talking to us in Latin, rather like Heby talks in French. Killingly funny! We were in fits – so was Hodge! She's jolly nice sometimes.*

And sometimes not. Miss Hodge could be quite frightening, although I admitted on another occasion *She's not so bad as she looks.*

The Summer Term brought changes. Timetables, subjects and staff normally remained stable for the academic year, but this time an enforced adjustment had to be made. Miss Maden was missing from the beginning of the term and was described in the Diary as *having a rest for a month or two.* In fact, she was suffering from multiple sclerosis. If I had known how ill the unlucky woman was I might not have written the callous-

118

sounding comment that *Singing is far better without Miss Maden*. All I meant, though, was that it was better because *Every week we are going to have half singing and half listening to records. Today we had a piece from Handel's Messiah*. In the following weeks we heard a good deal of the *Nutcracker Suite* which I loved, the *Joan of Arc Overture* played by a brass band, and a recording, which had been broadcast on the BBC's Children's Hour, of hymns sung by pupils at one of the other schools where Miss Maden taught, the Royal Masonic Girls School. A series of substitutes, including Miss Hodge, helped Miss Morgan-Brown to cope with us, but occasionally Miss Morgan-Brown coped single handedly and proved to have a heart of stone: *Singing for half of afternoon. Stupid old Morgan-Brown made us stand all the time! Three quarters of an hour!* Fortunately, by mid-July it was announced that *Next term Miss Maden will recover and return*. She did, and things went back to normal.

The opportunities of listening to music would have been particularly valuable to me at that time because it was something we could not or did not do at home. I know we still possessed my parents' collection of records, classical, jazz and popular medleys, but either we had no gramophone or the old one we had was not working. I suspect that Mother might have avoided listening to those pre-war Beethoven and Mozart recordings on account of the emotional associations they would arouse.

* * * * *

Over and above every one of our teachers, and over every pupil of the school at this time, there spread like a great mantle that was gradually settling upon the building, forming itself to the shape of every corner and leaving no edge uncovered, the presence of the headmistress, Ruth Garwood Scott. The force of her personality had made such a dramatic impact on the very first day that some people were hardened against her from then on, but it was also recognised that the school needed the strength and determination that she obviously could wield.

119

Now throughout her first year she was engaged, as the Diary shows, in the task of getting to know the school and the name of every girl. She paced the corridors and paid many visits, some prearranged, others unannounced, to classes.

Monday March 6 Miss Scott came to read and criticise our exam results.

Thursday May 25 Not such a nice art lesson to-day. Miss Sturrock was on edge because Miss Scott was expected and we were jumpy and couldn't work properly. Miss Scott didn't come.

Tuesday June 20 Miss Scott came into Geog. Miss Meir left and for a whole half hour she questioned us in alphabetical order on all different subjects. I was first with a science question.

She came to Latin and sat while we had a revision quiz. I think it was mean to waste our Geog. revision time.

Miss Ruth Garwood Scott

Wednesday September 20 Biology ... [Miss Bannister] showed us the knee jerk and Miss Scott came in as we were practicing it. She thought we were up to larks I think!

Friday September 22 Miss Scott came to see us at lunch break. Just told us not to grumble as a lot of work was done for us. She was dressed very nicely today.

My first personal encounter with her took place one afternoon in May as the form was marching along a corridor on the way to an English lesson. Sensing that she was behind us and catching up, we were maintaining an impeccable, silent single file. All at once she came alongside me and I felt a soft touch as her hand lifted one of my plaits. I turned my head to find her smiling and remarking what beautiful long hair. She said she hoped I would never have it cut and I think I murmured an awe-struck 'Thank you, Miss Scott' and 'No, I won't, Miss Scott'.

Her appearance was the first weapon in her arsenal. With her own posture she symbolised a backbone of self-discipline for the school. Very erect on high heels, striving to compensate for lack of height, she walked always with the same measured step, exuding dignity, and when seated she positioned her legs elegantly and held her head slightly on one side. The aquiline nose and dark brown eyes formed an impression of acute alertness, of nothing escaping her notice, of power. Soon, however, she was inspiring devotion as well as fear. Even in that early portion of the time she served the school, while I was still there, I witnessed this. She was on the threshold of joining the long line of remarkable women who had governed the Lady Eleanor Holles and she would be outstanding among them.

* * * * *

The sanctions which were meant to keep six hundred girls under control were remarkably few. The most minor of them was the 'order mark' – *Stupid old Griffiths in P.T. gave Vanessa and I order marks for not changing shoes!* – and then came the detention. This was more serious because it required parental involvement. You had to get the slip signed to show that your mother knew you would be late home on the given afternoon. For many of us this was the worst part about it: facing your parents with the facts of your wrongdoing. I can remember the feeling of inner, squirming embarrassment when I presented Mother with my one personal detention slip. It was for arriving late at school three times in a term, which to her was a far worse fault than bad work would have been.

A detention lasted the length of a lesson, beginning from the end of the normal school day. Whatever form you came from, you sat through it in one particular classroom where one member of staff could supervise, though when we, the notorious Lower IV Y, were given a form detention I imagine we had to have a room to ourselves. You were given some set

121

piece of work to do, for the system of writing out lines was not used at LEH.

The cause of that form detention, by the way, was that on 3rd March we had provoked Miss Bishop because *We kept talking in separate groups when we should have been listening to other people's questions.*

But as has been seen from the Diary, detentions did not always deter, and the next step up in the scale of severity was to be sent to Miss Lacey, the Deputy Headmistress. Miss Lacey taught chemistry and was the senior science teacher but lacked the automatic gravitas with which Miss Scott was blessed. She was plump, bespectacled and ungainly, with an unlucky readiness to flush and on the whole looked motherly rather than commanding. Nevertheless, an inner integrity must have given her a firmness that was camouflaged by her physique, for she was well-respected, and to be 'sent to' her was no light matter. What happened to you when you were there I cannot say, but she was certainly kept busy in 1950. Of necessity, the entire burden of the worst disciplinary problems would have fallen to her lot while Miss Scott was new.

Eventually a time came when the ultimate penalty was to be sent to Miss Scott herself. (She was still 'Miss Scott' while my schooldays lasted but was addressed as 'Miss Garwood Scott' in later years when another Miss Scott came to teach at the school.) As far as I can remember, the girls condemned to this terrifying experience had to wait in the corridor outside her office. They would have to stand there until she happened to emerge and discover them. The room was located in the centre of the school and a rule of silence prevailed at all times in that area, giving it an air of sanctity and danger.

No expulsions and no suspensions took place that I can recall while I was at LEHS. Corporal punishment was never dreamed of – or should I say it was never considered. Poor Miss Firth may have dreamed of it. Just twice that I can recall a crime was committed that had to be brought to the attention of the whole school. Only one of them occurred in 1950, a suspicion of theft. *Friday May 26 Missed French. Had to turn out desks and satchels because Jane Burly, U V A, has lost some books. This is nasty as it's so near exams and she's a genius.* On second thoughts, though, maybe it was not theft but mere loss that was suspected, for even our troublesome form would hardly be likely to steal the books of a genius three years above us. The other incident, perhaps a year later, was a case of scurrilous graffiti in the lavatories. Lessons ceased for an afternoon and the school was summoned to the hall where with all the force at her command Miss Scott thundered against such unspeakable horror.

Miss Scott did not add to the structure of punishments but she did inaugurate a new reward, the Excellent. For this too you queued outside her door in the hushed corridor, usually on a Friday morning, to show your worthy piece of work and receive a word of praise.

* * * * *

Out of the pages of the Diary there now come voices loud and clear to which I was deaf when I wrote it. They are the voices of the women who taught us, whose inner lives, whose true feelings were never taken into account for a single moment in my consciousness. They were merely teachers, a special breed whose existence consisted solely of carrying out a job with children as its objects. They were 'decent' or 'rotten' according to what they said to *us* or what they made *us* do. At the age of thirteen we, I at any rate, did not question what lay underneath the surface. They were well-liked on the whole but I feel now that I was totally thoughtless of them.

Reading now the quotations I have used, listening with adult perception to those voices from the classroom, I can sense the tensions and the tiredness that the staff might have been suffering and can also tell with sudden clarity just what hard work we were. They were ordinary human beings. How did they feel? Did some of them wish they did not have to teach? How unhappy did we make Miss Firth? How nerve-racking was it for Miss Scott to get through her first days of the enormous responsibility she had taken on at one of the foremost girls' schools in the land?

Of course it was not all strain and pain and I suppose we would have acknowledged that they were as glad as we were over our successes and enjoyed as much as we did those lessons that went tripping along with good humour and enthusiasm. Yet we would have been amazed to learn that the people we pictured solely in the one narrow context where our paths met, be it French grammar, or theorems, or hem stitching, were also interested in the theatre and the arts and literature and were generally informed way beyond the narrow field of the subject they taught. Stereotyped by us chits as old maids if they were unmarried (the majority were), criticised for the way they dressed, grumbled over and made fun of, they could, in fact, boast richly cultivated minds, qualifications to daunt the faint-hearted and an average level of intelligence that was quite formidable.

A considerable separation was maintained between their professional and their personal lives. I don't think familiarity had to be actively discouraged, I think the lack of it was part of the accepted way of things, but it meant that quite mundane details about them could intrigue us. Even to learn the Christian name of one of them was to have uncovered a secret, an intimate and almost guilty fact about her. *Miss Maden's other name is Sybil!* Only in the Sixth Form would a girl perhaps be on more equal terms with a member of staff.

Young and good-looking mistresses tended to have an advantage in popularity, especially if a fiancé in the background gave them an aura of romance, but even then they married discreetly in the holidays, came back as a 'Mrs' with a new name – *Wednesday April 19 Back to school. Miss Lovelace now Mrs Rogers* – and left before a pregnancy became visible – *Friday December 1 Mrs Rogers was absent and she will be for the rest of the term.* No public announcement was made about a birth when it happened, apart from a notice probably months later in the school magazine, and none of them ever brought a baby back to show us.

* * * * *

An important factor in the maintenance of school discipline was the part played by prefects. To a thirteen year old, the prefects were almost equal to adults. We would usually straighten up, quieten down and stop misbehaving if somebody hissed, 'There's a prefect coming!' On the other hand, they were open to a certain amount of teasing and provocation.

You were liable to run into prefects when you were less likely to meet teachers, on the way home, for instance. A prefect on the bus would check any noise or rowdiness and make sure you kept your hat on. Generally, I would say, they were obeyed, and a junior girl seriously reprimanded by a prefect would take it to heart.

The hierarchy consisted of the Head Girl supported by two Headmistress's Prefects, appointed by the Headmistress herself, with about twelve prefects and a number of sub-prefects elected by school and staff at the beginning of each year. Their insignia was a rather impressive medal hung on a red ribbon. At break times and after lunch, when the entire school was streaming out in the same direction, the prefects stood on point duty in the corridors, constantly calling out, 'Keep in line!' 'No running!' 'Quiet please!' To compensate for their responsibilities, they could relax in a little room of their own furnished with armchairs.

* * * * *

The thwack of tennis balls against racquets is one of the most evocative sounds of summer, inseparable from the scent of new mown grass and distant calls that carry through an open window of 'deuce', 'thirty love', or 'double fault'; and if you are a female whose sporting life ended when she left school these small sketches form a composition which is entirely to do with schooldays. The reader may detect in this reverie the implication of a purely passive enjoyment, of listening to other people playing tennis, yet for that summer term in 1950 the Diary was witness to a burst of honest effort and enthusiasm that should have had better results.

It was only our second season on the courts at school so that aspirations were still open, future attainments fluid, not fixed as in subjects we had been learning for years. There were, of course, exceptions among us, people who were already well out in the lead, and among the most prominent players in our form was Pamela. She was voted Games Captain on the first day of term and I think some of her keenness rubbed off on me.

Wednesday May 3 Pam brought an old tennis raquet of hers. It's very small and light, but she's given it to me to practise.

Friday May 12 Smashing tennis. I can return quite well now. And at home that evening: *Did prep in garden, or, rather, did ⅔ Algebra and rest tennis. Practiced against wall by garage.*

Monday May 15 I'm crazy on tennis!

Tuesday May 16 Stayed to tennis after school.

Wednesday May 17 Tennis. Practised service, my weak point. Miss Miller helped me, told me how to improve. She gave me an old school raquet to take home and ask if I can have it. 7/6d. Mummy said yes.

Thursday May 18 New raquet is fine. Nice and springy. Played at lunch and break ... getting better.

Monday May 22 Glorious weather. I practised awfully hard in tennis lesson. Terribly hot and tired afterwards.

Wednesday May 31 Very hot. Used new tennis balls in break. I bought two on Sat. String bag I tried to make didn't work very well!

... and so on. I cannot imagine stronger evidence of an utter dedication to the game than spending my own money on balls and making a string bag to carry them in, but it was all in a good cause, for Pamela had been having coaching and I probably thought that if I spent enough time at it we could make up foursomes at the weekends without my disgracing her. On Sunday 4th June part of this objective came true. Pamela came over and, with Tina Fermor, who brought a fourth girl along, we played on the courts in the police grounds at Imber Court. *Nice game*, I commented, but whether I made a fit partner for any of the other three I doubt.

That day marked the peak of a brief, bright episode in my sporting life, after which all went downhill. There had never

126

been a hope of keeping up with Pamela, and it was not long before a hint of my real level of aptitude crept into the Diary entries, although my spirit was not yet daunted: *I'm glad I'm not in the rounders team. People who are not, could play tennis! I'm getting better at scoring but my service needs improvement. We lost all games I served.*

Shortly after this the spell of fine weather came to an end, I stayed home suffering one of my bouts of throat infection and then the exams began. By the time tennis was mentioned again in the Diary a couple of weeks later, the position had become all too clear: *Had tennis. Four of us always go together 'cause we can't really play. We do have fun.*

It is something, I suppose, to see that the word 'fun' appears quite frequently in the Diary in connection with my sporting endeavours, but no, I couldn't really play, and finally, after all those hours of practising at home and staying on after school, the story ends on a sad note of disillusionment: *Thursday July 13 Watched tennis matches in afternoon. So* <u>terribly</u> *boring! I thought, as I knew more about tennis, it wasn't going to be bad, but oh, dear!*

Meanwhile, however, some of the sporting euphoria had spilled over into rounders and for this too I joined the girls who stayed after school. *I love these little informal games,* I wrote. *I may stay every week now.* I think those little games were actually informal to the point of being unauthorised and they were stopped. All they amounted to was a half dozen of us bowling a few balls and running a few rounds in the middle of the field, using our satchels already packed with homework as the bases, and since this formed no part of the official timetable it meant we were not supervised and not going straight home as we should have been. But the remark (above) about being glad not to be in the rounders team referred to an earlier lesson and shows that I *had* had my moment of glory, even if it had come and gone rather swiftly! *Friday May 19 Had rounders. I was made an 'extra' for the second team last time – I'm not any more.*

As to why I did so badly at games, one might theorise that it was a handicap to have a mother who never could play, but the theory does not stand up. Mummy could not paint either, but this had no effect on the artistic ability of Jan and myself. Besides, she was always encouraging. She wanted us to enjoy sport and she wanted us especially to be good at tennis. Like piano playing, it had potential as a social asset as well as a lifelong pleasure. I was given encouragement also by teachers and by having a friend like Pamela who jollied me along while I showed any spark of interest.

But all was not lost. There remained the third activity of the summer term at which I might accomplish something and indeed it gave me a day of triumph greater even than being an extra in the second rounders team. I learned to swim.

Friday June 2   Went straight to swimming after English. How lovely to view again that clear turquoise deep (though I kept in the 3 foot). Faye and I kept together and helped each other. I nearly did a stroke!

Friday June 9   Swimming. Miss Griffiths says I can nearly swim. The small group of non-swimmers have great fun. We all hold on to each other in a ring and kick our legs out. Water nice and warm. 73°F. The pool where these rather infantile jinks were taking place was the public open air swimming bath at Hampton to which we either walked in crocodile or were taken by coach.

The weekend after this I had a chance to swim in the river. *Went with Fermors to the river. They've got a boat. I swam properly with help of a rubber ring. Smashing!* Unfortunately this seemed to result in another sore throat, and back ache too, so I missed the next lesson at Hampton and for various reasons it was the 30th before we were taken down to the baths again, but this turned out to be the great day. *Swimming directly after break. I did it! I waved wildly and kept up though I didn't move forward much. Oh, I was happy! I must do it properly next time.*

But the new found skill had only a fragile hold. The following week: *French after break, then swimming. Went in coach again. Water very cold. Did not swim or anything important this week,* while the final visit of the term to the Hampton Baths was the occasion of the Swimming Gala, at which people who didn't move forward much were not entered in the races.

128

There remained a last opportunity that year to build on my tiny bit of expertise, to prove it is true that once you can swim you never forget how to do it. On holiday later in the summer I managed to swim in the sea. *Then it was, at 4.30 p.m., I swam! Suddenly, surprisingly!* It sounds as if I just relaxed and let it happen, which would have been the best way to have tried it all along.

* * * * *

The school playing field was huge and, apart from that brief flirtation with tennis in the summer of 1950, I spent most recesses and lunch hours out there on the grass rather than on the hard courts playing formal games. Sometimes three or four friends would stroll around chatting, sometimes a larger group of us would play he, chain-he or 'release-io'. To pick the first person to be he, we would dip, all players standing in a circle with their fists held out while one of us thumped every fist in turn with her own and chanted, 'One potato, two potato, three potato, four. Five potato, six potato, seven potato, more!' Another dip went:

'Dip, dip, dip, my little ship,
Sailing on the water
Like a cup and saucer.
O-u-t spells out and out you must go
Because the king and queen say so!'

The cry for giving in when you got a 'stitch' or were out of breath was 'Pax!'

The traditional, seasonal children's games that one reads about such as hoops or spinning tops, belonged to earlier generations as far as we were concerned, and some, like hopscotch, would have been impractical without a paved surface. There were always plenty of skipping ropes to be seen, however, and, even without the seasonal changes, a craze would spring up for a particular activity. The craze often involved some hobby or craft like French knitting (requiring

129

an empty cotton reel with four pins stuck in it) or making pom-poms by winding wool round and round old cardboard milk-bottle tops. Cat's cradle was endemic, and back in the late 1940s, when plastics were the new thing, we could buy packets of multicoloured, thin plastic strands and plait or weave them into – well, into plaits, I suppose, or just long strips, woven for the sake of weaving!

Anyone who wanted a more obviously useful hobby could apply for a school garden. Little plots ran alongside the path which crossed the field.

There was a great cult of horses. Most of us, when in the junior school, had built camps in the hedge and played 'families'. From an early age, several of these families had been formed exclusively of the girls who loved riding, and these were the ones which survived into the teenage years. Indeed, they became if anything more intense. Dozens of imaginary horses cantered around our field every break time. They took part in gymkhanas, were groomed and exercised and led back to their stables. Sometimes a girl who simply had to have the feel of actual reins in her hands would bring a sock horse to school as the next best thing to a real pony. This creature consisted of a stuffed sock with eyes, ears and a bridle stitched on, all tied to an old broom handle.

Over the years we gradually became more sedate. We walked and talked instead of running around, or in dry weather simply sat on the grass. We were not encouraged to work during our breaks; we were supposed to be getting fresh air. If you were not keen on this idea, there were legitimate reasons for staying inside. Every form had its library day once a week and there were club meetings (the Literary Club, the Art Club, the History Club, the French or German Club and the Christian Union). For my own part, I could often find some excuse for staying in the art room.

* * * * *

Mother's great endeavour was drawing to a climax. July was her final month at Hampton Training College and it was packed with hard work and with cogent emotions: the elation, the deflation and the poignancy associated always with one's last days as a student, at whatever age.

It began on the first day of the month when, despite its being a Saturday, Mother had an interview for the teaching post she most wanted. Her first school practice had taken place at Molesey Secondary Girls' School and the headmistress there, Gwenllian Davies, evidently impressed, had assured her of a job and urged her to apply as soon as she was qualified. Her official employer, however, would be Surrey County Council, and accordingly she had to attend the interview at County Hall in Kingston.

Left everything to go to Kingston for Mummy's interview. Jan and I looked round shops and had to wait an hour for Mummy because the horrid old Education dame kept her waiting. Then she insulted her and turned her down. If I could ... OOH!

Our rage on Mummy's behalf, almost more than the Diary could express, and the frustrated longing to strangle the silly, witless woman who'd rejected her were probably less than the downheartedness of Mummy herself in the knowledge of facing yet more obstacles and having to start all over again in the application process. The principle challenge fired at her during the interview apparently was 'You send your daughters to school in Middlesex!' the bone of contention being not so much that we were at a private rather than a state school, as that we were in the wrong county. Mother was applying to work in a school in Surrey and lived in Surrey, but while Jan and I crossed over the border to go to LEHS her county loyalty was in question.

Happily, although I have no record in the Diary of exactly when it happened, the decision was changed. Mother went on to teach in Molesey Girls' School for the rest of her working life and we sometimes wondered in later years whether the horrid Education dame's bad temper had been a deliberate interviewing technique and a test of a candidate's doggedness. Not being so detached at the time as to see it in this light, Mummy fell victim to a headache next day from the strain.

The following weekend she still had work to hand in,

because I *did some lettered labels for Mummy's folders. She hopes to finish all essays this weekend.* But I think the staff had already made their assessments. On Tuesday the 11th she came home with the news that she was best in her group, and the

Mother with group of staff and fellow students at Hampton Training College, 1950. Mother on left end back row.

next day came the crowning splendour. The Diary burned with pride: *Mummy is <u>BEST</u> in the whole <u>COLLEGE! BEST</u> of 180 women! <u>MY</u> mother! No-one else's, <u>MINE</u> is <u>BEST!!</u>*

So it had all been worthwhile.

And now the college launched itself on one of those frenetic bursts of effort that typically celebrate the end of a course, however short it may have been, almost outweighing in use of energy all the previous months' work and making a top heavy finale to single year's study. But the open days, the drama (Mother was in a play), the musical performances and the social events of that month, with the students' families thronging the college to see them all, spun their own energy from the release of pressure and, of course, there was the need for that last close union with the community they had grown into, so intense and strong, and the metaphorical embracing of friends and companions before separation. Mother must have felt buoyant as she took Jan and me around.

Monday July 24 Mummy's third Open Day. We're going this time. Mr. Keif took us in his car. It was wonderful! First we looked round at all the work. Mr. Greensmith (Tutor) showed us the Drama room. Saw Mummy's folder. All the other rooms were super! The models, books, pictures, maps, folders. Lovely little shops for infants. Then we had a little tea and watched P.T. There was a manequin parade. Last we saw Bartered Bride, a play. We were being introduced to tutors and girls all the time. Mr. Keif took us home in his car. We arrived at 8.15 p.m. approx and had a large supper.

Soon after this came the last day of all. *Friday July 28 Rather grey this morning but it turned out fine later. We went to see Mummy off. She got a lift from Miss Simpkins, her tutor. I can't believe that over a year has gone since she started training.* And at the end of that day: *Mummy was very upset that she's left Hampton for ever.*

I think Mother was a star to all the tutors and they probably knew her well enough by now to appreciate the huge exertion and will-power that lay behind her success. Arnold Keefe (I believe this is the correct spelling) was taking her out and coming to the flat quite frequently at this time, giving his professional artistic encouragement to Jan and me; I don't know whether there was a strong attachment between them but the relationship outlasted the end of the term by a few more weeks.

What Mother now needed and what all three of us were longing for was the holiday we'd planned. We were going to stay in Torquay with Auntie May. What a wonderful prospect – but then a shadow fell. *Had letter from Auntie May. She's*

133

looking forward to having us. 1½ hours later Gagga rang up. She's not well, may not be able to have us. Oh, I hope so! Torquay, the sun, sand and palm trees! I hope she gets better.

So it hung in the balance.

* * * * *

For Jan and me the end of term was ten days earlier than for Mother.

Monday July 10   Pamela and I are absolutely agreed that school is dragging most terribly.

The exams had been more fraught than usual from my point of view and pessimistically on 5th July, as the results came in, I was writing: *I am declining rapidley. I got 59% and was 11th for Biology. I really hoped to pull up on Needlework but I was only 18th with 58%. My average is only 70.5% and I haven't a chance of being 2nd now. Sonja is better than I.*

One unexpectedly pleasant result, however, improved matters and raised the average. *Came into form-room this morning, found large crowd round Miss Tame. Art results. Worst exam I thought I'd ever done in Art, but best result – 86%, 1st. Oh, I'm thrilled. Art matters more than anything to me and it's now my best mark.* This being the day when we also heard about Mummy's college results, I summed it up at the bottom of the page in the Diary as *Wonderful day! I'm 2nd in form with Sonja. 75%.* So Sonja and I were still vying with each other, not for leadership as in the previous term but for attainment, and Janet Barrell was still invincible at the top of the class. I have kept the drawing I did for that Art exam and my judgement of it is the same as in 1950: it did not deserve such high a mark.

While our exams were marked in percentages, the system applying to our homework and to the overall grades that appeared in our reports was an alphabetical one, A, A-, B +, B, B-, etc. A was the highest mark you could expect for even your best efforts, since A + was held in reserve for something utterly outstanding and the D grades were the lowest. They were pronounced as English letters of the alphabet, not the Greek *alpha*, *beta* and so forth used by some other schools.

* * * * *

The following excerpts from the Diary cover a miscellany of minor occurrences of the previous three months, both at school and at home, that fit into none of the main sections of this narrative but might add an extra dash of flavour:

Friday April 21   Got posture stripe in rounders lesson. Got order mark in Geography! So near beginning of term, too! A posture stripe was an award for having a straight back and walking well, but it came under the aegis of the P.T. department and hence I had been astonished to have gained one. Great importance was attached to deportment, not as one of the social graces or 'accomplishments' of young ladies, as in the past (for such a superficial educational concept would have been beneath us at LEH!), but for the sake of health and to avoid round shoulders. The stripe took the form of a little red enamelled bar about an inch long, worn like a brooch on one's blazer or cardigan, as were the monitress badge and any other insignia. The next rungs up the ladder were the gym stripe, a little blue enamelled bar and, ultimately, the purple games stripe.

Monday April 24   New girl arrived. I had to look after her and take her round to lessons. Juliet hasn't done any Latin. Don't know how she'll get on in exams.

Tuesday May 2   Was late, with Pamela, for school again. We must watch our step!

Thursday May 4   Missed half of Art. Mrs. Somebody-or-other came to give lecture on 'Save the Children Fund' – how it works, etc.

Finished David Copperfield in P S. [Private Study]

Wednesday May 17   Bees in Biology. They're most interesting! It's amazing how they live and build and work.

Monday May 22   Don't feel like going to school. Never do on a Monday now.

Wednesday May 24   [Empire Day or Commonwealth Day,

135

as the Diary prints in brackets] *Sang 'God Save the King' in prayers.*

Thursday June 8   Went to Literary Club meeting in recess. There will be an expedition to Merchant of Venice in open-air theatre, London. I am going to go.

Friday June 30   John came over. Gave us sweets and money. Played with us and had a good old discussion.

Monday July 3   No science results yet. Back to normal lessons now – splitting water into elements.

Tuesday July 4   Missed Latin to see cheque being presented to Hospital. Money we saved is being used on pictures for Children's Ward at St. Mary's Cottage Hospital. This was the school's local, long-standing charity. I believe the money was raised by a contribution of one penny per girl per week throughout the school, a collection that had been going on ever since I went to LEH. We called it 'Hospital Cot Money' and by now the sum of £137.10.0 had accumulated. It was to be spent not only on pictures but also furnishings for the ward, and I think one particular bed was especially 'ours', with a plaque over it publicising the fact.

Every form raised money over the year for a charity of its choice as well as this, with a monitress appointed to gather in the pennies. A list published in the school magazine of the organisations that benefited during 1949 and '50 includes, as would be expected, a number of charities for children, animals and the blind, for OXFAM and for cancer research, but also the Merchant Navy Fund, the Greek Relief Fund, the Zenana Bible and Medical Mission and, coming closer to home, the Darby and Joan Club, Hampton!

Sometimes as a special collection we would send off sacks of clothes, shoes or toys to one of the poorer nations (I don't think we had started calling them 'the third world'). On one such occasion, a girl of about Jan's age was seen in tears on the bus, clutching an old floppy doll. She had outgrown it so her mother had made her bring it to give away but she still loved it.

Friday July 7   At 5.40 p.m. Mummy and I went off to school to play. Scenes from St. Joan by Shaw. Very well acted by

Upper IV. Met Miss and Mrs Clark there. Lovely walk back at 10.0 over field. Scores of beetles buzzing around. (Who Miss and Mrs Clark were will be explained in the next chapter.)

Saturday July 8   They have sweet cigarettes at Sheridans! We got some.

Watched Molesey Carnival go by. Same wonderful excitement as first band came in sight. Usual ribbons, waggons, toddlers in lipstick and pretty girls.

Monday July 10   Started imperfect tense in French ... Had lots of smashing team games in hall as it was wet in P. T. lesson.

And from then on we were winding down to the end of term:

Thursday July 13   No lessons today. I wasn't pleased about missing Art to watch rounders matches but I didn't mind missing Latin, etc ... Stayed in form room till lunch packing books, drawing, etc.

Friday July 14   No lessons today either. Very long list of notices at prayers. Miss Scott must be looking forward to hols. She kept making jokes and giving us time between notices to talk and 'shake ourselves'.

Monday July 17   We had some lessons today ... Attended to form business and went to see flowers in 3rd period. Patty arranged a flower competition. Our form got a second class ... Miss Miller and Miss Meir are leaving. I don't mind about Miss Meir but fancy losing Miss Miller! Just when she'd got to letting me off those somersaults too. We gave them their gifts in prayers ... Watched a play by Lower VI. Not bad.

Until finally:

Tuesday July 18   The last day as L IV Y. Last day with Miss Tame. Last time we'll see a good many people. Spent morning collecting autographs. Got most of prefects, Miss Miller, Miss Meir and others. Janet Worthington's leaving us. Got last things packed. Messed about in form room. Had long recess.

Breaking up Prayers was last thing ... Sang end-of-term hymn [this was the classic 'Lord, dismiss us with thy blessing'], *shook hands with Miss Scott, cheered Miss Tame and the form, then went home. I'm rather sad, but our form has had a bad reputation this year.*

Now 8 weeks holiday!

137

5

AUNTIE MAY

The long holiday began with housework and shopping. With no necessity to get all our provisions in on a Saturday, I was content to go pottering off to the shops nearly every morning and generally it was the first task of the day, to be followed by any cleaning work that I had chosen or been asked to do.

'Chosen' may sound somewhat unlikely but both Jan and I must have been quite willing to wield a broom and duster otherwise we would not have devoted so much time to it as a hobby. *Thursday July 20 Shoo came early. I did some shopping. The first holiday job, just as last year, was to clean Rose Cottage. We washed and brushed the floor and seats, cleared away the litter, put a picture up, and a vase of roses on the window sill. Then we drew in there and played snap.*

Rose Cottage was, in fact, cleaned several times, far more than its tiny dimensions justified (it must have been about seven feet in diameter) but if children's play is a preparation for adult life, Jan and I were teaching ourselves to be efficient housewives and, appropriately enough, it was in this little feminine nest of ours that we were called on one day to defend the position of women. *Monday July 31 Jan went to Paul. Richard and Pat there.* [I'm afraid I don't remember this particular Pat.] *I cleaned Rose Cottage and put fresh water in the 3 vases of flowers we've put there. After a while (I knew it would happen!) Jan and Pat fell out with the boys. They* all *came round and I became the centre of a tense argument. Boys were better than girls, they said. We girls argued the opposite. After a lot of shouting the matter was left and we all played together.* Although full details are not included in this Diary description,

I remember the incident and I'm afraid we girls came off the worse. The row came down to a tit-for-tat sort of contest with both sides trying to score by firing off the names of famous people. The trouble was, we girls could think of only two great women, Florence Nightingale and Queen Mary, so we didn't do a lot of good for the feminist cause. Heaven knows why those were the only two; we should have been able to quote a few more than that.

On the matter of housework, however, we were not just little Marie Antoinettes out there in our *Petit Hameau* pretending to work like grown-ups. No sooner had Mother broken up than she plunged into an orgy of delayed spring cleaning and though, of course, she had to undertake by far the major part of it herself, we had to put our hands to it as well, or at any rate I did, for I cannot say how much Jan at her age was expected to do. Most of my chores were probably in the nature of support and back-up, relieving Mother of some of the secondary jobs like making breakfast and lunch, drying up, sweeping carpets, tidying up, and mending. All these are mentioned in the Diary.

I cannot be sure that my labours were thorough enough to be of real value but my guess is that I would have been too thorough and therefore terribly slow. On one of my school reports Miss Tame had written that I 'should try to be a little more brisk', and I can picture myself painstakingly sorting the contents of a drawer, for example, and taking ages to decide how best to rearrange them. Chores *did* get done, though. In the Easter holidays, over a period of three days, I had cleared out the bottom of the dresser in the dining room, where toys and books tended to be chucked higgledy piggledy, concealed by a curtain, which *took me all morning and some of afternoon. Polished it and put things tidily. Looks quite a lot better now. There was a whole sack of rubbish* – and then tackled the 'blue cupboard', another hideaway for books, papers and painting gear. I had also cleaned the oven.

By the summer it was imperative to get the dirty little flat cleaned up while Mother was between college and teaching and before we went away (for we *were* going to Torquay). It was the only possible time to do it. The first step was to get the chimney sweep in; logically no cleaning could be done till he had been. I was sent round to make the appointment with him and he came on 31st July, his main duty apparently to sweep not an actual chimney but the boiler, the great 'White Rose'. This done, Mother in three separate attacks scoured the dining room, then I helped her clean out the kitchen cupboards and wash china on the Sunday and she and Shoo did the hall the next day. She must have felt pretty worn out but would have a good rest in Torquay.

It was at some time during these pursuits that I gave a yelp and fell through the kitchen floor, or at least one leg did. The lino had been concealing the fact that the boards were crumbling with rot.

For Jan and me, pocket money was not job-dependent and therefore we did not earn extra by doing more work. No doubt we sometimes had to be nagged into usefulness but on the whole I think we had the sense to know that with Mother working as she did, we had an obligation to be helpful, and I am positive that we would not for one second have had the impertinence to say, 'Can't Shoo do it?'

* * * * *

Like a true housewife, I dressed myself up one afternoon and left work behind to visit a friend.

Miss Clark was the sweet-natured young woman who had been my tutor before I entered Lady Eleanor Holles. Private tutoring was the rather fine-sounding form of education offered under the aegis of LEHS to girls who were either preparing for the entrance exam or who had been accepted for entry at the start of an academic year. For the latter, it avoided the difficulty of finding yet another school for just a single term, as would have been my case after we had moved to Molesey in April 1946. When I was Miss Clark's pupil that summer, I was with one other girl and it was utterly delightful. We went to the house in Hampton where Miss Clark lived with her mother and had lessons in an upstairs room. We were

140

there for the mornings only because all we needed to do was to keep up with our sums and our reading, learn a few poems and colour some pictures.

I loved the Clarks' house because every part of it seemed to possess a sort of story-book charm and tranquillity, from the garden full of roses where we played in our mid-morning break to the large kitchen with its rugs, rocking chair, dresser and ticking clock, and completing the picture there was Mrs Clark, a white-haired, smiling Irish lady like a fairy godmother.

Miss Clark liked to keep in touch with former pupils and about three weeks after Mummy and I had met her with her mother at school when we went to see *St Joan*, she sent a postcard saying, 'Do come to tea with me this Tuesday, Madeline, if you can. I should love to talk to you again'. And so ...

Tuesday August 1 Washed a bit and put on my other new frock with lemon stripes ... At 3.30 I started for Miss Clarks. Arrived at 4.0. Old Hollesite there, Lucy. Also Ann, an old pupil of Miss Clark's. Mrs Clark brought tea on the verandah. We all played table tennis after. Lucy went home. Miss C., Ann and I went on golf course. Played table tennis after. Home at 9.0.p.m.

It was Miss Clark who had also been my last piano teacher, the one who was too kind to enforce the discipline of constant practice.

Finally, for Jan and me a visit to the fair on Hampton Court Green on Bank Holiday Monday (the first Monday in August as it used to be then) marked the true end to our scrubbing and sweeping and a taste of holiday spirits. *About 3.0 we went (just Jan and I) to the fair! What crowds! But what fun! We tried penny-rolling, Hoopla. Then I went on a round-about, Jan did not want to. Had a candy-floss each, Jan bought a balloon, paper umbrella and bubble stuff. I had paper hat.*

We were flush with money because a couple of days before we had had a windfall. *Oh, joy! Wonders! £1 each from Uncle John to spend at Torquay! We three were just talking and saying how little we'd have.*

All excitement was now focused on Torquay itself.

Tuesday August 8 – The last day! Packing of course. I was

running back and forth all day, shopping, getting last minute oddments that we'd forgotten till then. First it was things for tomorrow's lunch. We're having it in train. Lots of cigarettes to last Mummy whole three weeks.

All things laid out on our devans. Cases dusted, labels stuck on. Shoo was ironing yesterday's wash as hard as she could. Line was full of clothes airing. At last all was finished, all except things like brushes and combs. Jan and I got two drawing books. Hope we haven't forgotten anything.

(The purchase of all those cigarettes is a mystery and I cannot explain why they could not be bought in Torquay.)

Wednesday August 9   The great day! Weather was bad this morning. We set out in pouring rain ... Mr Shepherd drove us to station with all our bags ... Train to Waterloo, taxi to Paddington. The porters, the fear we should be late! Of course, we were alright, bought some magazines and settled down. Then off!!!

Sun came out and brightened our journey. Had lunch on train. Mummy had packed it. Ivy, lady who knows Auntie May, met us in car. Auntie is in bed. High tea and early to sleep for us!

It is a wonderful journey to the West Country, particularly after Exeter, when the route traces the coastline around the estuary of the Exe and on to Dawlish and Teignmouth, with the train cutting through the red rocks and emerging to display the seashore almost at the edge of the tracks. And at the end of the long day there we were at last, in that most pleasant of houses – Woodstock.

Woodstock stood at one of the curved corners of Carey Park, an oval-shaped 'square' of large and secluded houses in the Babbacombe side of Torquay. The house was beautiful in its proportions and comfort. It dated from the nineteenth century but one felt it was built not so much to be imposing, as houses like 7 Wolsey Road were with their rather grand, stiff frontages and flights of steps, as to be homely and easy. It was a generous house in its assortment of rooms, with extra rooms for a variety of purposes: a morning room, an apple storage room, a study, a conservatory; and then, if you opened the door at one end of the hall, you found yourself in another

Auntie Margaret in Carey Park, Woodstock in the background

hall, another half of the house. The Bokhara carpets did not extend into this half but it boasted almost as many rooms again, with pantries and larders, kitchen and scullery, laundry room, and china cupboards, shelves, tables and sinks everywhere for a variety of culinary purposes while on the floor above, separate again with its own passage running parallel to the 'main' landing, was another set of bedrooms, the servants' quarters. We three all loved it.

The Woodstock garden was not large. It was quite informal, and rather than being divided into a distinct 'back' and 'front', it surrounded the house and consisted mostly of lawn and shrubberies, with an opening in one corner leading to an orchard. This plan somehow gave a very sheltered, tranquil feeling to the place.

When we had last seen Woodstock, Auntie May and Auntie Margaret had both been living there, Uncle Alfred having died in 1940. May had Gagga's blue eyes and white hair and a strong, fine voice with the Welsh accent slightly more evident than in his. She used to sweep her long hair up in abundant silvery coils and pin a huge black, stiff bow at the back. On the top of this she would balance her glorious hats, piled with ribbons and ostrich plumes, and she always wore loosely-tied sashes round the waists of the frocks that she still had made in the styles of the 1920s, the way Alfred had liked them.

At the time of that most recent visit of ours, at Easter 1949, the two sisters and the house were looked after by three staff: a housekeeper, a maid called Lilian, who had a lovely rolling

143

Devonshire accent, and a gnarled old gardener whose Devonshire accent was so rich that Jan and I could not understand him. The aunts' lives were busy with civic and social activity, but the house was half-empty compared with what it presumably once had been. Auntie May had been brought there as a bride, contented, by all accounts, to join the household of her parents-in-law. Like Gagga, she had left Wales when young to find work and by the time Uncle Alfred met her she had become the headmistress of a school in Southall. The marriage took her into an altogether more affluent mode of life in a wide social circle. Alfred Harris was a difficult man, a hypochondriac and a frightful snob who wished her to avoid letting their friends know that she

Auntie May

had once worked for her living as a teacher, but he did not disdain voluntary work. He became an alderman on Torquay Town Council, and May served as a councillor for the local ward of St Marychurch as well as being involved in social work and many charities, which helped to utilise some of her energies. The couple remained childless, however, and as often happens in such cases, they became fond of one favourite niece, Valmai. I doubt if Uncle Alfred would have made a very tolerant father, but the presence of a quiet young girl who could be petted and cosseted and would blossom when removed occasionally from the harsher, poorer background of her upbringing to the genteel comforts of Woodstock (like Fanny Price?) – this was a pleasure, and to May a joy. Indeed, they had wanted to adopt her.

It might have been on account of Mother's newly diagnosed

144

Woodstock in the 1940s

heart weakness that they first invited her there, for she was about twelve at the time, and from then on she would go down sometimes at Christmas, sometimes in the summer, always afterwards to cherish the most loving and happy memories of those days.

What a sombre difference Mother found there now. Auntie Margaret had gone and Auntie May was more seriously ill than we had realised. She lay in her four-poster bed and the only other occupant of the house was an elderly companion-housekeeper, Miss Strickland, who seemed resentful over the turn things had taken since she was engaged and was probably afraid of what more might be put upon her.

Whatever letters or messages had been exchanged before our holiday was confirmed had not revealed Auntie May's true condition, and if she herself had misled Mother, who can blame her? I can understand how much she would have wanted to see Mother again and how reluctant she would have been to put us off and disappoint us. She would have kept hoping to recover enough to take us out and about and, indeed, may have been encouraged by her doctors to believe our visit would do her good.

However, I do not think Jan and I were aware of any gloominess in the atmosphere. We three were on holiday, we were near the sea, we would enjoy ourselves. We couldn't wait to get down to the beach and, luckily, on our first morning we woke up to glorious weather. That first day and our last day, as it turned out, were two out of only three days in the entire three weeks when it did not rain. *Now we're here and it seems quite ordinary. It's marvellous, all the same ... After breakfast*

145

we went to get rations and shops. Auntie May gave us some money! At last to the beach! On the way we bought a huge rubber ball, besides a lovely bucket and spade each! Changed into costumes and went into water at once. Played with ball, jumped over waves, caught crabs, and built castles. Had picnic on beach. Tide came in in afternoon, beach too crowded. Went to sit in gardens on cliff, looked down on harbour. Light tea when we got home, dinner at nearby hotel at 7.0.

So, an idyllic start. Just the sort of things we had wished for and there were indeed many trips to the Abbey Sands in all, but also many hours when we could not go out. It proved a godsend to have brought Jan's little dolls with us, her 'three little dolls with real hair' (predecessors of Barbie), for which we had both been making clothes before coming away, and whose lessons and tea parties now occupied the two of us through the wet periods; and just as at home, we got out into the garden at every sunny break.

Auntie May arranged for us to go riding a couple of times. Jodhpurs were lent to us and we *trotted down little lanes and walked on road. Had a good fast canter once.* We had learned to ride a year or so earlier when for a time our father paid for us to have lessons at a stables near Hampton Court.

Several of Auntie May's friends asked us to tea and usually a lift to and fro in a car was laid on somehow on these occasions. Our hostesses were mainly elderly ladies but the visits to them were not boring. They offered the chance to see another attractive house or cottage, with another garden to explore, other books to look at and another little acre or two of Devon to admire.

We had some worry over finances, for one night, less than half way through the holiday, I lay wide awake between 2.0 and 3.15 am calculating that *out of 30/- each over 15/- has gone!* And this even though Auntie May had paid for the replacement of our big rubber ball when it burst! The wet weather probably caused more trickling away of cash on comics and sweets than if we had been on the sands all day long.

The Diary gives an indication of the inescapable responsi-

146

bility Mother found herself burdened with during the holiday. *After breakfast,* reads an entry five days after our arrival, *(which Mummy gets early now so we don't have it with Miss Strikland) Jan and I went into the garden ... Soon Jan and I went off to beach. Mummy was busy so she came at one o'clock with lunch.*

Monday August 21 After [lunch], we thought Mummy would not be able to come. Ivy, who comes most afternoons, couldn't come, and Miss Strikland doesn't like being left with Auntie. But she said she'd be alright, so Mummy came.

Friday August 25 Made bed, had hair done, etc., very late, as Mummy was seeing to Auntie.

These incidents, and a number of others when Jan and I went out alone because Mummy was tied to the house, are open to a variety of interpretations. They give an impression that Miss Strickland was quick to shift the duties of tending the sick on to the relative who had conveniently arrived on the scene, but these may not have been her duties in the first place. Mother apparently could not get on with her and I would judge that the separate breakfasts were a way of avoiding her, while as to Ivy, I cannot say whether she was a kind friend helping voluntarily or whether she was being paid. Mention is also made in the Diary of 'Matron next door' but it reads as though she was simply the neighbour, not employed to nurse Auntie May but either a retired hospital matron perhaps who happened to live next door, or else the principal of a nursing home in that house, an establishment pointing the way most of the residences of Carey Park would go in the future, Woodstock included. Neither do I know to what extent Auntie May was incapacitated at this stage and needing to be nursed, but there is an implication that she could not be left alone. It could have been that she quite naturally wanted Mother to be with her in preference to anyone else and wanted her company as often as possible in those three weeks, looking on her almost as a daughter.

Auntie May's illness was, of course, cancer, similar in type to that of Auntie Margaret, affecting the liver and lungs, although in her case the primary tumour had been excised some years before.

Woodstock 1997, converted into a private nursing home

* * * * *

Since Miss Strickland obviously could not be imposed upon to cook dinner for us, arrangements had been made for us to go down to a private hotel at the other end of Carey Park each evening for our main meal. Needless to say, in our rather difficult circumstances, this was often the highlight of the day and the subject of food took on even greater importance than usual in the Diary. Almost every menu at the Penrhyn is recorded and very good they were, as shown in the following few samples.

Chicken and veg., soup, ice cream with raspberries!

Rabbit pie for dinner. I was hungry, so after plums I had jam tart. (This one, incidentally, came after we had already had rolls and ices at a snack bar on the way home, with Devonshire cream.)

Had some water melon, which I had not tried before. Lovely!
I had extra Yorkshire pudding instead of cauliflower. (Gladys the waitress obviously spoiled us.)

And the rather odd mix of *Tomato soup, peas, bacon, heart, roast chips, Swiss apple.*

* * * * *

Just as an incidental, I noted in the Diary that Princess Elizabeth was 'safely delivered of a princess' on 15th August and I said I had been hoping the baby would be a girl.

Two visitors came to Woodstock while we were there. The first was Auntie May's doctor who had also been a friend for many years. It had been one of Auntie May's philanthropic activities to be involved in the late 1930s in helping European refugees to settle in this country; in fact, she was appointed the organiser of her area and Woodstock became a centre where people could stay while being found a permanent place. A young doctor and his parents came over from Czechoslovakia. His name was Jan de Winter and he was able to establish himself in a Torquay hospital, eventually becoming an eminent cancer specialist and in later years setting up the Cancer Prevention Foundation in Sussex. He was always grateful to and extremely fond of Auntie May. At the time of her illness he probably would not have been her regular, local practitioner, but would have been coming to see her as a specialist and a friend. He came twice that August and spent a long time with her, also bringing presents and chocolates for us. He was tall and good-looking and I thought he was *awfully nice.*

Our other visitor was Gagga. He came for three days towards the end of our stay and I can imagine how thankful Mother must have been to see him even if their conversations together were undercut with sadness. With him we drove around the bay one evening seeing the fairy lights, walked on the downs and went to Abbey Sands.

By the time he left on 28th August our holiday was nearly over.

There had been two bright events that compensated for the

149

dull days. *Friday August 18   Auntie May has some very nice books in the lounge. Jan and I found five volumes of Nature Study. Auntie wants me to have a book which was presented to Uncle Alfred. She said she wants me to have it more than anyone.* She sent me downstairs again to find it, and when I had done so I wrote: *It is lovely. It is signed by the author.* The book was *Dance of the Months* by the Devonshire writer, Eden Phillpotts, consisting of a set of twelve stories describing the landscape and encounters with local people on Dartmoor. It had been presented to Uncle Alfred as one of a limited edition of 1,000 copies.

The second event left Mother and Jan and me wondering if we had witnessed some sort of magical illusion: *Had a fine afternoon. Took the shortest bus ride possible (1d is the dearest and only fare!) To Meadfoot. The waves beat against the rocks. Reminded me of Scarborough. We had drink and cakes then climbed up Daddyhole Plain (enchanted name!) in the rain. The colours of the sea! A rainbow spread into the sea and over the trees and an old fairy galleon-like ship came slowly across the bay! Beautiful!* We tried later to find out what such a ship had been doing in the bay but no one appeared to know anything about it and we could see no mention of it in the local newspapers, so we half-convinced ourselves that it was truly supernatural.

We left Woodstock and Torquay on 30th August. *It was simply pouring when we woke! What a busy morning. Packing, rushing, collecting, returning, good-byeing. As usual, after a holiday, we seemed to have twice as much to bring home as we took with us. We HAVE got twice as much!*

Gave Auntie and Miss Strikland a present, said goodbye to Matron. Finally, hugged, kissed Auntie May, swallowed a lump and went.

There was some talk of our returning at Christmas but I am sure that when I swallowed that lump in my throat as I kissed Auntie May goodbye, I knew I was not going to see her again.

Hers was a dreadfully prolonged and lonely death, with almost everyone who was close to her so far away. Medical procedure decreed in those days that once you were ill you were put to bed and discouraged from exerting yourself in any way. Only in the following couple of decades did the custom of centuries begin to change, for until then the only place in which a sick person could be kept comfortable and warm in most households was in bed. As an illustration of the strictness with which invalids were kept confined, I quote a note added to my birthday letter from Gagga a few weeks later: 'Please tell Mother that Auntie May herself came through on the phone. Nurse had given her permission for her to do so'. So there she lay in the four-poster bed, evidently by this time being professionally cared for and needing permission even to go down to the hall in her own house to use the telephone.

She died on 14th December.

* * * * *

One more active social event was crammed into the short time left before Mother went to work. Mother's school friend, Ivy (sometimes nicknamed Barney), her husband, the genial Bart (another nickname – from the surname Bartholemew) and their small children were making the arduous journey from Romford to spend a day with us.

Saturday September 2   Did shopping. Lot of cakes to get as Ivy, Bart, Richard and Mary are coming tomorrow. Jan and I haven't seen them for 2 years! After, I did some more to my story book.

Sunday September 3   Not-too-good weather today. But lovely otherwise. I wrote more in my story book most of the morning.

Auntie Barney, Uncle Bart, Richard and Mary arrived about 12.30 p.m. Mary starts school tomorrow. Richard can nearly read. They liked Jan's puppets. After lunch Shoo came. Mary helped clear things away. Shoo and Jan washed up. I read story to Richard and gave him the book. Showed Mary and Richard the garden. Saw 4 cats out there! I had a little read myself and after a lovely tea (jelly, blancmange, gooseberries, cakes, evap. milk) we all watched Muffin on T.V. They went at 6.0.

I was told recently by Mary that she still remembers that day.

* * * * *

And then five days after the end of the holiday which had been a strain rather than a rest for Mother, *Jan and I saw Mummy off with kisses and wishes and love,* launching her into her new life as a teacher.

* * * * *

Who was then the lucky girl who had another holiday, one which though brief turned out to be 'better than Torquay'? The Diary by this stage shows a marked improvement in handwriting from that of the early months and the small pages are tightly inscribed with neat, tiny writing giving all the details, so I think there is no better way to transmit the excitements of my adventure than to copy them word for word. It began in the afternoon of the day Mummy started teaching.

Tuesday September 5   Mummy's had a good day. John came for me after tea. Shoo packed my few things. I'm going to Southend for the first time! Lovely journey in the evening. Saw Jupiter coming out, stopped at a lorry drivers' café for a cuppa! Got there about 9.30 p.m. so John took me round to see lights on pier and shrubbery. Marvellous! I'm sleeping in John's room. He lives with Kitty and Mansell. Kitty has two dear little cats! I was in bed very late.

Wednesday September 6   This is the day I've been waiting for. John generally eats out but this morning he and I had a fruit breakfast. I washed, etc. after and out we went. Got bus into town and from the pier head took the little train to the end. 1¼ mile long pier. Longest in the world. Royal Daffodil is the boat. At ten she started. With us. It's a largish boat. Can hold 2,000! John and I wandered round, had a drink. Southend grew distant, finally disappeared. Sea was calm and sky blue. Stopped at Margate. Soon after that we had lunch. Should have had it before. We had to queue, but got cold chicken. While eating, we saw the point of the trip – France! Cruised around the coast about an hour. Saw place where Channel swimmers start, Dunkirk, Normandy beaches. Golden sand, hardly any people.

152

Miriads of huge jelly fish! John and I sat out on deck. Wind grew strong on return journey. Had a good talk on radar as we saw 5 destroyers with radar guns. Home at Southend at 8.0. What a wonderful trip. After a cuppa and game with cats went to see lights and torchlight procession. They were better than last night. Home at eleven.

Thursday September 7 Slept fairly late today. When I was ready we went out, said goodbye to Kitty and cats first (Mansell busy) as we leave straight after. John likes just the sort of things I do. Not-very-well-known, sometimes-snubbed sort of café. We had a super breakfast in a place near. It started grey but as we drove along the sun came out. Stopped at a snack place and had a cuppa. Ate apples and read, discussed things with John while driving. Went via East End of London. Stopped at Whitechapel Academy and looked in. Some work very good, some fair, some poor. Drove along Thames Embankment to Houses of Parliament. Got out, tried to look round, but they are only open on Saturdays. Stopped about 2.0 at Tate Gallery. Had a lovely lunch and looked round. Saw William Blake's pictures. They're marvellous! John bought me a couple of cards to add to my collection. Arrived about 4.45 at Nan's. They gave us salmon for tea, Nanny showed me her new frocks and came to Olwen's with me. I nursed Julian, who laughed and 'talked'. Nan and Gag are pets. They are always glad to see us and give all their best things to us. We said goodbye then drove home.

A rich little interlude, packed with new experience, in which, as I clearly recall, the transport café and the coast of a foreign land seemed equally thrilling.

* * * * *

The next day, back at Molesey, I had a last minute rush to buy Mummy a birthday present. She wanted a powder compact and after searching further afield I came back and succeeded in finding one just round the corner. Shoo and Jan and I wrapped everything up, tied bows on the packages and placed them in the fruit bowl.

Saturday September 9   Mummy's Birthday! 36 years old. Jan and I brought her tea on a tray with the bowl of gifts. It did look gay with all the coloured crepe paper. Compact from me and ten cigs. From Jan: 6 cardboard plates and a propelling pencil. Shoo gave 3 pretty hankies and nice card ... 10/- from John and 10/- from Nan and Gag. Mummy was thrilled!

The last grains of sand were now running down through the neck of the holiday hour glass. I had just time for one overnight visit to Pamela's, where we exchanged our holiday gifts (she had seen a little more of France than I had and had brought me souvenirs of Brittany) and then I whizzed back home to join Jan in an industrious session of pencil sharpening, satchel packing and covering books with brown paper. We were ready for school again.

6

OH, GHASTLY DAY!

Oh, ghastly day! I proclaimed on Tuesday 12th September.
After prayers Pam and I bid a sad goodbye, for we're in
DIFFERENT FORMS! I'm in Upper IV A, she's Upper IV B.
Another thing is I've got Mrs Lequyer as a form mistress! And
oh! We have the GRIFFIN for P.T. There are only 12 old Y's in
our form, with 20 of those X's!

I poured out troubles and had a good old cry at home this
evening. Felt better after a hot bath.

The new academic year was off to an unhappy start but we
soon had to make the best of things. The fact that members of
our old form were outnumbered by almost two to one in the A
stream reflected the truth that as a whole we Y's had not done
as well as our unloved sisters, the Xs, but this we had always
known.

During school hours Pamela and I would hardly cross each
other's paths except at break time and could not even sit on
the same dinner table, but we could still travel home together.
Meanwhile, being set adrift, as it were, without my 'best
friend', I was designated to take care of our one new girl,
Maureen Wells, who therefore became my table partner and
with whom I got on well enough to keep in touch for many
years into adult life. Pamela too needed someone to go around
with and she became friendly with Cynthia Moore. Soon those
two and I had formed a threesome, strolling together at the
end of the day as far as Cynthia's house nearby in Hampton,
and again it proved to be a durable relationship. Maureen was
not excluded from this trio; it was just that she was a boarder
and so never walked home with us.

155

Perhaps the factor that presented the most enduring diffi-culty was that fate had appointed Madame Lécuyer as my form mistress for the year. Mime Lécuyer (not 'Mrs'), for so she was known, having a French husband as well as being a teacher of French, was a Scotswoman and of a rather sharp, impatient temperament. Her moods were unpredictable and she expressed them, often sarcastically, in her clear Scots accent with an air of deliberately flouting the principles of English reserve and English inhibition. Although she tried to be understanding when a girl needed help (as will be seen presently), the sort of dreamy slowness that I was prone to probably irritated her, and if I had not been good at French I think I would have had a very troubled time indeed with her. It may also have helped my case that through their common bond of Scottish birth, she was friendly with my best ally, Miss Sturrock.

Our second day of term was *another nasty day* and included a French lesson with her for the first time. *French with Lecuié is ghastly! She seems to have a grudge against all old Heby's people. Said my writing was shocking. It is sometimes, but I've got an A+ in the book.* The Diary itself shows that my handwriting certainly was shocking unless I put some effort behind it and, indeed, even those neatly written entries remarked on above, through the holiday period, gave way to the old scrawl again a few weeks later. The fact that Madame Lécuyer was right in this respect, however, did not make me feel any less sullen at having the fault instantly pointed out.

Our next French lesson proved a little more enjoyable. *Lequié in better mood and told us all her history of when she taught at Hampton Grammar* [our neighbouring boys' school]. *Apparently the boys sent a petition to the Head about her, but she won the case and they were subdued!* Such a revelation must have had us riveted to our seats but unfortunately the enter-tainment did not last and, without being able to remember the full tale behind this tantalising synopsis, I think it is safe to assume that the Hampton boys had been rebelling against Mme L's outbursts, for so many of the Diary references are along the lines of *Madame L. in bad mood. Kept shouting...*

156

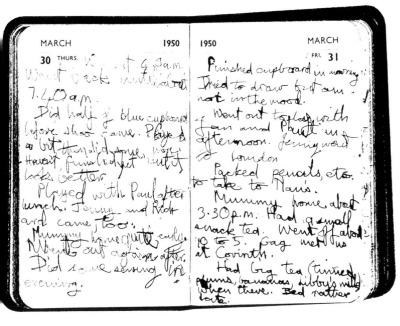

Shocking handwriting

Or: *Madame has got a voice for shouting, though she can't bear to hear us laugh even!* Possibly the story was told as a warning to us of the uselessness of any similar petition we might be contemplating!

In spite of the drawbacks, by the third day of term my spirits were lifting and I felt myself settling down. During the first lesson, which was P.T., we were weighed and measured. *I'm 6 stone 4¼ lbs and 5' 2¼".* Taller than Sonja! So Sonja and I were in contention again, this time in the physical race over height. Why it should always have been her I compared myself with and nobody else, I do not know and can only surmise that it was because we ran very close to each other in the various rivalries of school life.

Our form room was now on the ground floor, half-way along that limb of the building that would form the base line

Aerial view of the school later in 1950s with new science wing added to the E shape

of its 'E' shape if seen from an aerial view. Form rooms were always set out in a conventional arrangement with rows of desks facing the blackboards and the mistress's table placed to one side close to the window. The capacious oak desks were as rugged as ships' timbers and I believe that we still dipped into their inkwells with the traditional old steel-nibbed pens for our written work, in fact I have some recollection of fountain pens not being permitted until one was in the Sixth Form. They would have been considered too valuable to risk loss. There is a Diary entry, however, which puts this in question, when half-way down a page I change from ink to pencil and write *my pen's run dry,* but maybe it was only at home that I used a fountain pen. One thing I do know, which is that ballpoints were banned. They were bad for the handwriting!

The staff stayed in their rooms, we girls trooped around the school from lesson to lesson. When leaving the form room we carried the books needed for, say, the two periods after

1. Miss Broughton
   (School Caterer)
2. Miss Lacey
3. Miss Patterson
4. Miss Cooke
5. Miss Lovelace
   (Later Mrs Rogers)

6. Miss Hodge

7. Madame Lécuyer
8. Miss Sturrock
9. Miss Morgan-Brown
10. Miss Tame

11. Miss Davies

12. Miss Denney
13. Miss Hepburn

Some of the staff of LEHS in 1948. The group includes thirteen of those mentioned in the Diary.

Prayers, or the three periods between break and lunch, leaving all the rest of our property in our desks. At the start of each day we were meant to pile up the exercise books in which homework had been done on the shelf near the door and the book monitresses would deliver them to the teachers concerned.

The changes in our routine in that new term led to greater detail in the Diary reports about both teachers and the subject matter of lessons. The splitting into the A and B forms on the basis of ability became irrelevant in a way, since for nearly all subjects we worked in divisions. The divisions streamed the sixty or more girls of our year into three rather than two groups, so that there were usually about twenty in a set.

We still had Miss Tame for maths, for which I was grateful, and nice young Miss Brayshaw (I had a pash on her) for Latin, but for biology, English, history and geography we had a change of teacher. References have already been made to Miss Denney's history lessons, which were both super and smashing, and so too was geography now that Miss Meir had been replaced by a cheerful lady called Miss McKitterick with a rather flamboyant manner. *Geography with Miss McKitterick. She's quite nice but queer. She doubted whether we knew north and south but expected us to draw map of America off pat! ... She told us to make it neat and gay as possible. If it's only a sketch map you are doing, make it colourful, she said. Suits me! I like her.*

But not everyone met with such approval in the Diary. *Biology with Miss Bannister! She's barmy!* I declared. This condemnation was premature, however, for not only did Miss Bannister turn out to be a thoroughly likeable woman as our form mistress in the Lower Fifth year but she became something of a heroine by proxy when her brother Roger ran a mile in less than four minutes. She it was who was demonstrating the knee-jerk when Miss Scott walked in (see Chapter 4), and soon she was teaching us about the lungs, illustrated by a dissected frog, which I would have thought was interesting enough, but I wasn't satisfied. *I wish we could study the microscope and things under it like Pamela's form are doing,* I grumbled and then a few

160

weeks later we were doing exactly that, and peering at the spiracles of an insect. Perhaps what rather soured me was the fact that *I always get rather uncomfortable in Biology, sitting on those straight, hard stools, with no back.*

Meanwhile on the literary front *We have Miss Duce for English, which is a change. Miss Bishop was a bit soft. We are reading Silas Marner. Also we've a play book with the Coventry Nativity play in it. Poetry book as usual.* The poetry did not always provide great inspiration: *Read 'Dong with the Luminous Nose' by Edward Lear. Pretty weak. Apart from his lymerics I'm not keen on Lear.*

Where we had previously had physics as our only science lesson, with Mrs Rogers (formerly Miss Lovelace), which continued as before, we were now introduced to chemistry as well. For some reason physics had not appealed to me and on several occasions I had complained to the Diary of boredom. This term it received a better press, with reports of a *nice lesson* or *interesting experiments,* and once even a *smashing physics lesson* in which *We talked about radiation, discussed all sorts of interesting points and questions.* But it was chemistry which captured my keenest interest. *After break we had first chemistry lesson. It was with Miss Lacey and she's jolly D! We did some experimenting on our own. I was astounded when she said all the millions of things in the world are made of only 90-odd elements!* Later in the term I added: *Almost all the chemistry we do seems to be practical. It's rather fun. You have to concentrate and attend hard. If you don't you might set yourself alight with a bunsen burner!*

Our spiritual flame was kept burning by Miss Davies in the form of Religious Instruction. This was the same Miss Davies as mentioned in another context, whose good sense resulted in Jan's being allowed to have a dog. Her subject was one I found engrossing for its historical as well as its religious content: *R.I. was a good lesson. It was very interesting learning about Solomon's Temple.*

Art, on the contrary, was not perceived as essential to our higher mental development, and was being partly displaced, alas, to allow more time for the main scholastic subjects. So *by some minor tragedy,* as the Diary puts it, *we now get an art lesson only once every ten days.* Miss Sturrock suggested that I should *take a Saturday morning course at a Wimbledon place* (which I can only presume was Wimbledon College of Art), but later in the term at the parents' meeting she told Mother she thought I was losing interest. As far as I can remember, this was not the case, indeed *Wonderful art lesson!* is one of the most frequently recurring phrases in the Diary, although I seem to have lacked the initiative to sign up for the course at Wimbledon.

In contrast to our diminishing art lessons, the domestic sciences were expanding to include cookery as well as needlework. Half a year would be spent on each, swapping with the other group in the middle of the spring term. *Monday September 18   This afternoon we were split again into cookery and needlework groups. I wanted to do cookery but I'm not. However, we're making blouses and there are lovely flowered patterns of material to choose from. We have to find our own* [paper] *patterns. They'll cost 7/6d.*

We were still with Miss Patterson but tray cloths and aprons were things of the past and it was time for some serious dressmaking. A week later I duly took in the paper pattern I had bought. To my amazement, it caused great hilarity in the class. Without giving a second thought to the matter, I had chosen a pattern for a child, with a picture on the packet of a little girl jumping playfully, wearing her blouse, whereas everybody else had a Junior Miss pattern, giving a bust measurement where mine had a chest size and bearing a sketch of a sophisticated young lady modelling the garment within. Strangely enough, I didn't mind being odd girl out in this way and it did not occur to me to feel foolish over it. I was only surprised that the others considered themselves so grown up. Perhaps it made me reflect vaguely that childhood might not last for ever, but I got on with making the blouse and liked it none the less for its being childish.

For sheer drama and suspense, however, none of the academic or creative subjects of that term, even French, could match our P.T. lessons, and it was Miss Griffith, the Griffin (to whose name I consistently added an 's' in the Diary), rather than Madame Lécuyer against whom we were locked in rebellion. Two separate threads are clear in the Diary: one, my personal resistance to gymnastics and games and the other a solid refusal by the class as a whole to avail itself of an innovation provided for our benefit – lovely new showers, installed during the long holiday.

Among the woes of the first Ghastly Day was our introduction to the showers. *We had a* [gym] *lesson but spent time seeing showers. No-one wants to have showers but there they are; we're very lucky, they told us.* They had been fitted into a corner of the changing room next door to the gym and we viewed them with suspicion. But we were instructed to bring towels the next week, which made the solution very simple. We would all 'forget' our towels – and this was what happened. *None of us but two brought towels for showers.* Round one to the Upper Fourths.

Now why should we not welcome the provision of such a seemingly pleasant facility? Why would we not be glad to wash away the sweats of exertion or to luxuriate in hot water after playing out on the frozen field? The trouble lay in the way the showers were designed: they were communal. They consisted in fact of several water sprays within one large cubicle.

I have spoken previously of our shyness in connection with sexual frankness and this was one more example of the 'frank' generation of our elders attempting to impose their healthy and liberated views. It must have aroused in Miss Griffith the utmost impatience to see how ridiculously self-conscious we were about nakedness and probably she was baffled too by the fact that we minded it so much in front of other girls, all of the same age, not strangers but girls with whom we were growing up together like sisters. But these instincts were stronger than she'd bargained for and she hardened her campaign.

Oddly enough, though lacking all athletic prowess, taking a shower was one aspect of a games lesson that I could accomplish, and through the strong family ethos of the above mentioned healthy attitudes, which made it shocking to be shocked by and shameful to be ashamed of the naked human

163

body, I suppose I was less coy about nudity than many of the others. I was not one of the two scabs with their towels who broke the picket line that first time, but a couple of days later, presumably after increasing pressure from Miss Griffith, I was among the first few into the notorious cubicle. *We had showers after lesson. Undressed like lightning, skipped through and turned around while warm water sprayed all over you. Then a quick rub down and dress. I loved it!*

Yet overall, the Griffin lost the battle. By mid October *I had a shower with about seven others,* I wrote, stating significantly *We only have them now if we want to,* and soon it became *Only seven of us have them, same lot each time. Miss Griffiths says they're lazy,* I added, meaning the ones who didn't. *I think otherwise,* I concluded, so I must have sympathised with them despite being quite a keen showerer myself. Eventually, when the seven was reduced to five, she decreed that if there were not at least eight of us next time we would not have showers at all. I don't think the rest of the class was moved in the slightest by this threat, and no one stepped forward to strip and plunge in for the sake of their showering chums.

Running parallel to all this was what you might call the Saga of the Somersaults continuing from the spring term, in which Miss Griffith and I were now engaged in one-to-one combat. Miss Griffith frightened me, sturdily striding round the school in her short divided skirt, bare legged and ready for action at all times, and I perceived her as far less forgiving than Miss Miller, far sterner and more able to compel me to do the things I dreaded. But, strange to say, this rather daunting woman almost lost this battle too. It was a battle of wills but my fear was greater than her force, for the Diary entries now offer an interpretation that never occurred to me at the time: that she unobtrusively used to let me off.

The term began with what now sounds a somewhat pompous but was at the time a heartfelt avowal to do well at P.T. *Thursday September 21 P.T. first. Did not do anything nasty and it was a jolly D lesson. I think I'll try hard to do difficult things, be light, quick and springy. Then perhaps she'll like me.*

164

A week later this resolution was being tested to the limits. *She's started something – handstands over box! I wasn't in the team that had to do it but my turn will come.* Handstands were even worse than somersaults because you were poised the wrong way up for longer.

There followed a respite for a week or two during which I was absent through illness and was then furnished with a note from Mummy that left me sitting smugly on the sidelines. *Thursday October 5   Back to school. P.T. first. Still doing handstands – but not me! Mummy put it in note that I was not to do Gym for rest of this week. I had a nice time watching. Enid Tozer, who fractured her arm when she slipped in the showers, sat with me, so did Pat Bush.*

(There was no suggestion, incidentally, that Enid's accident had any bearing on the shower controversy.)

But after that there came a series of lucky escapes almost too good to be fortuitous. *Was just about to go up and do somersault when Miss Griffiths said pack up. How glad I was!* Repeatedly, the same thing happened, even though others were not so fortunate: *I missed handstand, though Griffin made Margaret Edwards do it*, I wrote on 17th November.

Finally, however, she must have decided I could not get away with it indefinitely and one day towards the end of term my world turned upside down. *Thursday November 30   We did somersaults over bar. I did it with three people helping me and a bit of struggling.* I expect the whole class came to a standstill to watch this comical and clumsy performance, and what a mystery it must have been to those who were naturally agile. My body did not look as if it was made to behave like a leaden mass, but the last bemoaning cry of the term proves that it was: *Oh, Gym. I cannot use a springboard. I don't know why; everyone else can.*

So much for being light, quick and springy.

Meanwhile, alternating with these painful efforts was the almost greater suffering of outdoor games. Nerves and the weather made a torturing combination, and pitiful cries are uttered in the Diary. *Tuesday November 7   Games, oh, horrible games! I just froze! Tried to run after the ball but waving sticks scare me. Netball was not much better.*

165

Tuesday December 5 Lacrosse. I've never had such an agonising lesson. It was so bitterly cold! We came in, some of us, to get warm for 10 minutes, then went out to netball. I don't see the point of playing in freezing cold.

As these quotations illustrate, for a single awful afternoon each week we indulged in our two main forms of merry schoolgirl frolics, netball and lacrosse, one after the other. It got the worst hour of the timetable over and done with in one go but it was only made endurable if you were paired against a girl whose sporting level and inclinations were similar to your own. Hence a number of derogatory insinuations about some of my friends – for instance: *Tuesday October 24 Netball first. Was against Pat Bush, so I didn't do badly! Tuesday November 14 I was next to Sonja again and we shared my cardigan. Lacrosse was awful.* With hindsight, of course, it is not hard to see that while huddled under one cardigan we cannot have been keeping very active, so it was hardly surprising that we felt the cold.

There was just one lighter moment in the term: *Tuesday October 31 It was so funny in lacrosse. I was goalkeeper! All dressed up in those funny pads! I spent all the lesson getting in and out of them!* I wonder if this was a sample of the dry sense of humour that I'm sure Miss Griffith possessed or whether she simply wanted to see how I would make out.

Whatever was in her mind, it can't have been as harsh as I imagined. Maybe something of that 'try hard to do difficult things' policy with which the term began, showed through, but at any rate, for her own reasons the Griffin marked me out for further encouragement in the most astounding way. She awarded me a blue gym stripe. I did not keep it long – one term or two perhaps; but on the very last school day of 1950 when the end of term lists were read out by Miss Scott it was like being given B+ for Effort. I was well content. The effort had been patchy and had largely failed but I *had* made it and this at least was acknowledged. Jolly D.

* * * * *

166

Tuesday October 3   My birthday!! 14 YEARS OLD!
*I woke about 6.15.a.m. Jan woke later and at seven Mummy
came through. Gifts were in white tissue-paper on tray. Had
cards from Jan, Mummy, Nan and Gag, Aunties Lizzie and
Ettie. Nan and Gag, two Aunties and the Shepherds all sent me
ten shillings. Jan's present was a blue torch. Mummy gave me
two – note paper and envelopes and 'June Roses' Morny talcum
powder. She's taking me to Kingston soon to buy a skirt. I had
my first set of oil paints from John. They're super! 3 brushes and
a Mahogany palet! Sootsy gave me sweets, Sandy and Alishan
gave 1/-*

I was ill in bed with a sore throat and all the usual
symptoms and enjoyed luxuriating the day away in Mummy's
bed in the sitting room, with a cat curled up on the covers,
more presents arriving from upstairs and the treat of a box of
ice cream sent by a friend of Mummy's out of sympathy with
my invalid state. When Shoo arrived she *filled the room with
flowers and lit a fire,* and Mummy brought home melon and
cakes. In the early evening a telegram came from my father
and the post brought more cards the next morning.

I can feel the atmosphere even now and the wonderful
comfort of that room with the crackling fire, and I was left
there for the night gazing at the soothing red glow when the
light was put out at nine o'clock after we had all had a game
of Monopoly.

In times of illness Shoo was our nurse and we had soon
discovered that it was one of her great strengths. The main
reason for this was that she was so sensitive to one's needs. She
knew when to let you rest and when to sit and chat. She knew
when to feed you and when to mop your brow. If you were
suddenly too hot, Shoo would come in to smooth out the bed
and turn the pillows to the cooler side. You would shiver and
she would appear with an extra blanket, feel thirsty and she
would enter with a drink. She was so good at it that we had
decided she was psychic and telepathic, an impression she had
created at the very beginning by intuitively being 'sent' into the
newsagent's where Mother had advertised for a home help.

The most remarkable demonstration of her powers took

167

place when Mummy had been teaching for a year or so and had been sent off on a two or three day course at Epsom. While she was there, she was taken ill quite suddenly, with a rather bad form of flu of some kind, having shown no signs of it earlier in the day. She set off for home, and as she got off the bus near Wolsey Road she found Shoo waiting for her on the corner. 'Come along now', said Shoo, with a supporting hand at Mother's elbow, 'Your bed's ready. I've put a hot-water bottle in it.'

She told us that it was from people's auras that she could read their moods or state of health.

As a believer in spiritualism, she could also detect the presence of the supernatural and would sometimes look up and speak to beings from the Other Side as if they had just come through the door. 'Come in, Friend', she said one day when all at once her Red Indian familiar joined us in the sitting room, but we thought she had said, 'Come in, Fred.' From then onwards I'm afraid we three sceptics adopted a rather jocular attitude towards the invisible guest, asking Shoo if Fred was going to be around tonight, but neither she nor he took any offence at this mockery.

Poor Shoo needed some spiritual comforts in her life and although I have no knowledge of whether she actually attended seances, I can guess that if she had done so, the spirits she would seek to make contact with would be those of the two little boys she said she had lost. This was one of the griefs she had suffered but of which she never spoke much even to Mother. Whether we even knew of this past tragedy in 1950, when she had been with us little more than a year, I do not remember. It certainly took at least this long for one other aspect of Shoo to come to light.

I don't think the problem had yet revealed itself when, because of her lonely situation and her devotion to us, we three decided to take her with us to Nan and Gag's for Christmas in 1950, and although I have a feeling she did not behave with perfect decorum the whole time while we were there, there was at least no major embarrassment. But shortly into the New Year of 1951 Auntie Kathleen employed her to

168

help at the Christening party of her new grandson, Denis's first-born, which was held at Wolsey Road, and this produced more obvious trouble. We meant well, but bringing Shoo further into our family and social life put on her a strain she could not stand, for these were occasions when alcohol was present and it was the drink that was Shoo's downfall. She would be offered a glass or two of wine, possibly sneak herself another, and soon be out of control. She would become loud and petulant and make low jokes. Through all the early months with us she had hidden her alcoholism by managing to stay sober while working and, fortunately, our flat would have been free of temptation, our sideboard innocent of any intoxicating liquor. But it was when drink was on offer or when there was money in her pocket, such as the alimony she drew from the Post Office or, I suppose, the wages Mother paid her, that she could not help herself. At weekends she went on the binge.

Jan can remember how sometimes, when perhaps she was only partially tipsy, Shoo used to drop in to see us and her behaviour would be just odd enough to mystify Jan and Paul. They would discuss it privately afterwards and try to work out why Shoo's speech seemed so extra careful and precise on these occasions.

The riddle of which came first, whether she had gone staggering down Gin Alley because of her broken marriage and other troubles, or whether life in India had brought out the addiction and caused the divorce, we were never to find out. She never did anything so bad as to be given the sack and was with us till we left the flat.

* * * * *

It had been a memorable birthday and one of my remaining mementoes of it is the letter that Gagga enclosed with the card from himself and Nan. I will reproduce part of it here because, for one thing, nobody ever wrote more loving letters and because it reveals too the constant concern of Nanny and himself for the sadness suffered by their bright and beloved daughter, Valmai. Although by now he mainly used to address me as Madeline, he had not altogether abandoned the pet name, Poppet, that I'd had since babyhood.

Darling Madeline,
                     ... The years are surely rolling on and our little Poppet has now reached the day when the 14th milestone has come into view. We are proud of our charming Granddaughter and we love her very very very much and we hope to see the day when she will have finished her schooling and grown into a fine young lady and a credit to her dear wonderful mother and to be the joy and pleasure of your mother's life. God abundantly bless our lovely sweet Poppet.
Heaps and heaps of love
        Gaga and Nanna

* * * * *

The birthday qualified me for an increase in pocket money and a later bedtime. Unfortunately. I have no record of how much pocket money I now earned nor how much it had been for the previous year. I had started receiving pocket money at the age of eight at a rate of threepence a week, after which for a while it went up by threepence a year, but by the time I reached about twelve the increments grew larger. An older child was seen to have more expensive requirements and the system was meant to provide graduated progress towards the almost adult sums that a girl would have to handle in her later teens. Thus at sixteen I would be receiving ten shillings, at eighteen twelve shillings and sixpence. But where I stood at fourteen I cannot say.

However much or little we had, for Jan and me the money was our own. We were not made to set aside any of it as savings nor did we have to pay for our sweets or books. At the same time, there were no impromptu handouts (other than those from the uncles and aunts), there was no cadging a bit more, no pleading for just another shilling to buy those lovely coloured pencils or that pretty little toy. I had once taken it into my head to produce a magazine to sell to all my friends (*The Cowboy Monthly*). For more than a year I churned it out by means of a simple printing set, but for this piece of capital equipment Mother had had to advance me the cost, namely 19/6d, nearly £1, and as a matter of principle I could not be let off repaying it in some trickling but fixed amount, out of the profits. She kept me to it strictly.

As regards the bedtimes, however, all is clearly stated in the Diary and confirms what I remember anyway, which is that Mummy, in common with Pamela's mother and the mothers of many of our friends, faithfully followed the recommendations of the Ministry of Health. This meant that, beginning presumably with infants being laid down at six o'clock, at some point all children would slot into the regime of going to bed a quarter of an hour later for every year of age, a steady advance which at fourteen took me impressively forward from a quarter past to half past eight.

Mother was almost a fanatic over sleep. It was to her a precious and elusive state, attained with difficulty and only too often dissolving away while you still craved more. Clearly her underlying ill health meant that tiredness was a constant and dominating condition of her life and made the sleeping routine of Jan and me a matter of major concern. In any case, as a good mother she had always respected the advice of the country's medical authorities and there was no disputing their rules about how many hours children should spend sleeping. They supported her own beliefs.

For much of my young life, therefore, we were sent to bed at those early times and as a consequence I developed a habit of insomnia. Well, perhaps that is an unfair claim, for it might have developed anyway, but what I remember is lying awake long after I had gone to bed. I was not ready for sleep.

Of course, Jan and I delayed, dragged out the bedtime process, yelled from the garden in response to the evening summons, 'One more minute', 'Just got to finish this go', 'Just got to tell Paul something,' and all the usual dallying excuses, and undoubtedly managed to stay up beyond the regulation hour nearly every night. But even then I would often be too mentally active still to fall asleep. I have the suspicion that Jan must have wangled relatively even later times than I did, because there should have been up to an hour between us and yet she was often awake when I got into bed. This I know on account of the talking we did and the stories I used to tell to while away the wakeful hours in the dark. Sometimes Mummy would hear our whispering and call from outside the door, 'Stop talking, girls, go to sleep.' Then Jan would drop off at last and I would be left with another occupation, straining my ears to hear what Auntie Kathleen and Colonel Gettins were listening to on the radio. They were in the drawing room directly above my head. The theme music of *Much Binding in the Marsh* would come floating down but, tantalisingly, the words were indistinct.

I was impatient with Mother over the bedtime business and irritated at the way in which she would suddenly peer at one of us, possibly in the middle of our telling her something we considered important, and say, 'You've got dark lines under your eyes, dear, you must have an early night.' I am sure the early night was hardly ever enforced and the dark lines were, to my mind in those days, invisible to anybody else, but it was a sort of formula, an incantation that reflected her preoccupation with tiredness and sleep. Later on in our teens, Jan and I reaped the benefit of her policy, though, because she would always let us lie in bed in the morning as late as possible.

In treating our illnesses, she believed in 'leaving it to Nature'. Although the Diary shows that she herself visited Doctor Bowling three or four times during that year, the closest he came to seeing Jan and me in 1950 was over the garden wall, for he was called in to us only when we seemed to have a seriously high temperature, with delirium, or when we had one of the recognisable childhood infections, in other words when we had caught something bad enough to need medicine. Our regular little ailments were allowed to run their course without the benefit of anything from the chemist apart from Vic's Vapour Rub, and even that could be substituted by Vaseline (a blob on the bridge of the nose to clear congestion).

172

Sore throats were soothed with lemon and honey drinks, first aid consisted of Germoline and Elastoplast and on one occasion Mummy was quite angry to learn that I had been given half an aspirin by another mother at a birthday party where I had complained of a headache. Auntie Kathleen remonstrated with her once for not possessing a thermometer so Mother did obtain one but it was used as if it were the thin end of a wedge, something that could lead you astray, and there was nothing like a medicine chest in the flat. She looked askance at such indulgences. And when I say she put her faith in the healing powers of Nature, I do not mean she turned to 'natural' remedies. If she ever came across such products as homeopathic and herbal cures, I am sure that she would have shunned them with as much distaste as she did the proprietary pills and potions that other people relied on.

It was not that she was unorthodox or sceptical of medical science in general. If medication were prescribed by Doctor Bowling she administered it correctly and completely. She dutifully attended school medicals and had conscientiously taken Jan and me as babies to the clinic every week. It was more the case, I think, that she distanced herself from taking on medical responsibility. She never wanted to know about the workings of the human body nor even how to count a pulse rate. Either you called in the experts, or you left it alone.

In some ways she was unwittingly ahead of her time. It is now recognized that aspirin should not be given to children and that minor virus illnesses can only be treated palliatively. She was working from different principles but the outcome was the same.

The one area of our health which was not normally left to take care of itself was that of our teeth. It puzzles me, however, that although Mother herself went to the dentist one day in the summer, Jan and I, according to the Dairy, apparently escaped the drill and the probe for twelve whole months. Maybe we went on one of those days when I didn't quite finish filling in the page. When we did go, I usually had to have a filling (although much later in life I was told that most of them would probably be considered unnecessary now) but no suggestion was ever made as to having our teeth straightened. We'd never heard of such a thing as an orthodontist and I think the hygienist too had yet to be invented. Occasionally a friend would tell us she had had to have a tooth extracted under anaesthetic and without batting an eyelid one could ask if she'd had 'gas or cocaine?'

* * * * *

I don't know whether the experience with the little girl's blouse pattern had planted some idea in my mind, or in Mother's, about my becoming more grown up, but the Saturday following my birthday found us in Bentall's in Kingston trying to buy the skirt Mummy had promised me without looking for it in the children's department, and we asked one of the assistants where we would find the 'teenage' clothes. The young woman looked at us blankly. There was no such thing as a department for teenagers, she had never heard of such a thing in the shop; she almost implied she had never heard of such things as teenagers, and it is true that as a separate species in those days they hardly existed. They were as yet merely a dust cloud on the horizon that would come galloping over the hill by the late '50s and in our use of the strange term Mother and I were about six years out of context.

Meanwhile, I still needed my skirt, and in the end, wondering how other girls solved this problem, we bought one in a small adult size, but so large, nonetheless, that I had to wear it with the waistband rolled over beneath my jumper. I was delighted with it and wrote in the Diary: *I've got a smashing new skirt. It's the first teenage long one I've had. Mummy's real birthday gift. With the 30/- I was given I got myself a lovely pair of fawn-coloured shoes to go with it.* I wore them the next day when Pamela came to us for what I suppose was a birthday lunch and a walk in Hampton Court Palace.

As I grew older, the peacock inheritance in my blood, vigorously encouraged by Mother, would bring out the intense love of dress displayed by many of my relatives, male and female, designers and wearers, on all sides of the family. In the

174

meantime, having new clothes was always a pleasure but I hadn't yet reached the stage where it was a vitally important part of life to me and I didn't yearn for more clothes than we could afford. To judge from the Diary, we bought something new for the summer and winter each year and, of course, made our old things last as long as possible.

The only aspect of our enforced thrift that I minded quite badly was having to wear clothes I had outgrown. I felt horribly conscious of the hem too high above the knees, the cuffs too short on the wrists. It mattered all the more as one grew older because above-or-below the knee was the distinction that separated the girls from the women, so I used to tug my school skirt down to get the last quarter inch of its length over my increasingly tall legs. I don't think I minded having to wear odd bits of our school uniform with 'civvies' during holidays and weekends, mainly the coats, shoes and summer dresses, for it helped to extend the wardrobe and preserve one's very best things. In Torquay, for instance, I must have been wearing my striped school dresses because it is mentioned that I twice tore the blue one on a nail; and a photograph of Pamela, Jan and me, taken near Hampton Court Bridge on the birthday outing referred to above, shows all three of us with our grey blazers over our best outfits. School clothing must have formed a high proportion of the total expenditure for all parents, yet I do not recall anything like a second-hand sale or a 'swap shop' having been organised.

It was important to have a 'best' set of clothes and that this should be quite separate from the things you messed around and played in. In theory, last year's best became this year's everyday, but from photos of this time it is apparent that some of the best dresses, Jan's velvet for example, would never be suitable for a lowlier role, so I don't know what happened to them.

In a time when there were no easily laundered casual garments such as track suits, the clothes that children were liable to make dirty had to be old and already half worn-out. On the other hand the laundry load was lessened and the concept of 'casual' carried surely to its limits when in high

175

The birthday photo – Pamela, Jan and myself.

summer we would skip around, even in the street, wearing nothing but our knickers. I had ceased to enjoy this freedom only about a year before the summer of the Diary. Within a short time, though, all our chests would be covered by a new sort of garment with a long and successful future ahead of it. This may sound improbable when you learn that it was introduced to us as a piece of school uniform, that we had to wear it for games lessons and that its neckline generally became so baggy that you needed to thread elastic through it, but such was the inauspicious way in which the T-shirt came into our lives.

Soon we were wearing our T-shirts with the new, shorter, square-cut shorts which replaced the old heavy 'divided skirt' style, and the T-shirt then had to hang freely outside the shorts and not be tucked into the waistband. This was considered very chic.

Meanwhile, during that season in 1950, all unaware of the grand fashion trends of the big wide world, it appears that I had a new blue and white jumper and shorts that I was wearing on 28th May, and two new frocks in July. *Mummy ... was home in the morning. We went to Kingston together. Mummy bought me two new frocks. Nice light cotton ones. One is lemon striped and opens all down the front, with two big unusual pockets. The other has a frill on the bodice. No pockets. Red and blue. Mummy also got an open-all-the-way-down frock. It's smashing. Light and dark blue stripes.*

The next purchases were the birthday skirt and shoes and then, at the end of October, we went searching for a coat. It was a Saturday morning again, and this time before tackling the shops we went to a photographer's studio. This resulted in the portrait of Jan and myself shown at the beginning of the book. *Went off to Kingston about 11.0 to have our photos taken. It was a nice place. I don't think I have come out very well. We are getting them for Xmas gifts. After that we went to get a new coat for me (much against my will). We found a smashing blue swagger with a cute little brown hat. Once out of shop, I didn't know whether I ought to have had it or not. I still cannot decide!*

The next day I must have been reassured, for we went on another walk in the Palace and I claimed to have observed that *a few people stopped to look at my new coat, in fact my whole outfit* – so clearly I felt very good in it.

Meanwhile, the week before, Nanny had already given me a coat of hers. Since at five feet two and a quarter inches I was now at least as tall as, if not taller than, Nan, I could wear her cast-offs and this one was a treasure, a pretty little swing-back tartan jacket. It would hardly have been warm enough to be a proper winter coat, though, so I would have had to have another one as well.

It was obligatory, of course, to wear a hat with one's best coat, but the cute little brown one, which was of a corduroy texture, was far too stylish to be perched on the top of two swinging plaits. Without cutting my hair, I had to pile it up in some more mature fashion. Enacting the same rite of passage as any Victorian girl, *I put my hair up* on the day I went to

177

Hampton Court with Jan and Pamela and the photograph shows that this meant winding the plaits round my head; but such an arrangement left no room for any hat at all, so it was not a permanent solution. Mother and I then worked out various ways of twisting the plaits up, one being to tie them into two rather strange lobes which hung at my neck like large pears. They used to come unravelled and fall down easily and, even if they stayed up, it was still difficult to find hats that could accommodate them. The obvious answer would have been to cut the hair. But we could not contemplate this for many years.

The new hat and coat – and Barnabas

I have talked about clothes and hair but until writing the final draft of this book I hadn't thought to mention make-up because it came so much later on. Those who are interested in such details, though, might like to know that I was first allowed to wear make-up on my sixteenth birthday. It had to be lipstick only, as Mother considered creams and powders to be bad for the skin. Mrs Fish, Pamela's mother, held the alternative view that powder was the thing for a girl to begin with since it was more discreet. My own opinion was that the skin was bad enough anyway, with its natural shine, so it wasn't long before I was dabbing on the powder like all the other girls, with Pond's Vanishing Cream as a foundation. It certainly was discreet, as it wore off so quickly that it hardly showed.

Jan happened to be going to a friend's party on that day of my sixteenth birthday and I was to go with Mother to collect her, so, of course, she had to be sworn to secrecy. When we arrived, however, I found myself the object of an orchestrated little act of nudging and giggling set up by Jan with her chums.

178

All I could do was to stand there grinning foolishly in my bright red lipstick.

To return to 1950, the final clothes shopping spree of the year took place on 22nd December, when John, Nan and Gagga had all sent us their gift money in good time for us to go and splash out on the sort of glad rags we might wear over Christmas. *Mummy, Jan and I went shopping in Kingston in P.M. John has given Jan and I £1 each and Mummy £3. Nan has sent 15/- for Jan and I each, Nan and Gagga have sent Mummy 30/-. So I have bought a pink cardigan, gloves and socks. Jan bought fur gloves. Mummy bought new blue skirt and blue cardigan. We are all very pleased.*

Bentalls, the department store in Kingston, was the heart of our shopping world and we nearly always bumped into school friends who came swarming there on a Saturday from all over north Surrey. While the little homely draper and the shoe shops in Bridge Road in Molesey gave off their candle-powered sartorial lights, Bentalls, encircled by its planetary satellites of Woolworths, Marks & Spencer and Kingston Market, exerted the great gravitational pull at the solar centre.

* * * * *

Late in November Mummy went to a Parents' Meeting at LEHS at which she mentioned to Madame Lécuyer that I was worrying about French. This apparently surprised Madame and as a result she spoke to me a couple of days later, *as she told Mummy she would. She asked me what I was worried about, told me I often looked pale and sad! I'm not to worry at all, she said, but to tell her about anything particularly worrying.*

This was indeed a difficult term and perhaps the signs of it were upon my face but feelings of depression had been occurring quite frequently throughout 1950. As far as I can tell from the Diary entries, there were no especially deep reasons for it, except that the previous year had been marked by the first strong consciousness of happiness that I can remember and now, maybe, my capacity for other emotions was developing. *Feel rather depressed. Don't know why,* I would write.

179

Sometimes the dismal weather, sometimes tiredness and sometimes incipient illness might have brought it on or else I was simply feeling cross and lazy, and admitted to being in a bad mood. One day when I woke up *late, tired and cross* it is obvious I was anxious about scrambling through some homework left unfinished from the night before, but as that had been the evening of Jan's birthday I need not have felt too desperately wicked about it.

In common with most of mankind, I was often smitten by 'Monday morning feelings', although they tended to melt as the day wore on: *Oh, Monday, horrid day! I did not know how I'd get through. I have got through, though, and quite enjoyed it.* Monday was actually a far less risky day of the week than Saturday and Sunday, and the great majority of attacks came at the weekends or on days off, suggesting that they arose from boredom, lethargy and lack of purpose. On the face of it I always had plenty of things to do, sufficient household duties and homework and enough leisure interests to keep me busy, yet there were many hours spent 'hanging around', not getting on with anything useful or definite. One particular morning in July when the summer holiday had begun describes it exactly: *I took some drawing in garden but did not do much. I felt like doing nothing but I wanted to do something, like I do when I don't feel well. I lay in deck chair for a while and then felt better.* A classic case of ennui. The following Sunday was similar: *Hung about reading till 12.0. Did not know what to do and I felt rather bored after lunch. Jan's friend Pauline came round. Those two played in dining room. I read.* And again one Sunday in November, with the nagging unease of having put off the wretched homework: *Lazy, nasty day to-day has been. Hung around and did not get down to prep. (which I'd left till to-day) till 11.30. Spent afternoon doing it . . .*

I half recognised that it would be better to have no choice other than to get on with work of some kind: *Friday June 16 Still tired and got a bit of a sore throat. Home again. Had an awful fit of depression while in bed this morning. Wished I'd gone to school to do some work. Exams on Thursday. I got up about 11.0a.m. Went in garden to overcome depression. Lovely and sunny.*

180

One example in December has the flavour of pure, artistic melancholy: *After lunch Mummy and I went to the ballet. I loved it but felt a bit depressed after. I felt awkward, somehow.* But the most apparently surprising instance of ill-humour was the one that came over me on the very day after my lovely Southend holiday, until you realise that tiredness was behind it again, compounded by twinges of guilt over things left undone. *Stopped in bed very late this morning. Mummy brought breakfast and I took it. I'm in that sort of mood for not helping others or caring much. I haven't done a thing for Shoo except lay tea table ... I suppose it's tiredness that's made me so depressed. But anyway I haven't written to Sonja and Susan yet.*

I think I am beginning to see those dark lines under the eyes that Mother talked about!

* * * * *

It was later on in the school year, when one day the class was asked to deliver a letter of some kind to our fathers, and I had to explain that my letter would have to be addressed to my mother, that Madame Lécuyer found out I came from a broken home. She called me up, I think, having checked through the pile of envelopes we'd handed back to her after filling in our addresses, and pointed to where I had written 'Mrs Appleby'. I was surprised that she didn't know why. At the time this happened there was a more immediate cause for unhappiness in my life but I saw the workings of her mind and the sudden understanding in her face and knew she had made the connection between the lack of a father and my looking 'pale and sad'. She probably thought it had only recently come about.

Since it was purely by chance that Madame Lécuyer had learned of my family circumstances, I think it unlikely that many of the other teachers knew of them either. I have stated near the beginning of this story that my father used to pay the fees when Jan and I were in the junior school and, in accordance with the normal practice, our reports were addressed automatically to him, although posted to 7 Wolsey Road, so that even the school secretary could have been unaware he was missing from our life. Indeed, the documents I still have show that it was in December 1950 that the last of the envelopes to R. Appleby Esq. was sent out, as if word was passed round by Madame Lécuyer in early 1951 and the name amended accordingly.

Among my schoolmates the majority would have assumed, as I assumed about them, that one lived with one's two parents and any brothers and sisters one happened to have. It would hardly be thought about, for fathers were the vaguest and least encountered of all those background figures, and the knowledge of, say, how another girl's father earned his living would arise only as an incidental part of becoming familiar with the lives of one's very closest friends.

For all I know, there might have been other divided families in my year, and certainly you would expect there to be several mothers widowed in the War, yet I never was aware of any. One girl had been orphaned by the bombing and was being brought up by an auntie, some of the boarders barely saw their far-flung parents, but divorce or separation were another thing altogether. They were extremely unusual.

I used to boast about it. On the few occasions when the matter did come up, I was proud of being so different from the average and when I imparted the information it often had a startling effect on the recipient. I liked to say 'I have no father,' for this was more dramatic than having one and simply not living with him, although I then had to climb down of course and explain more fully. It was not in any way a personal rejection of my father; it sprang from the same source as my pride in being a Jones-Appleby, with the qualities I thought the family possessed that made us stand out from the crowd. To be different, to be original, always seemed to me to be one of the main purposes of life.

Perhaps one of the reasons why I was able to adopt such a flippant attitude to the fatherless condition was that 1950 fell within a period of six years when Jan and I did not see him at all and his name does not appear once in the Diary. It meant that the new-formed unit of 'we three', which Mother from her inner strength had created out of the ruins of a family of four,

182

was consolidated. She imbued us with a sense of wholeness and security and it held firm, it was sound. She never spoke a word to Jan and me against our father; in fact, we were encouraged to admire him.

As to *her* feelings, I confess I was insensitive to them. All conscientious parents hide unwelcome emotions from their children. She hid her sorrow from us, and it is not always true that children are intuitive about the people around them. I rarely sensed the different thoughts that lay beneath a normal, smiling adult face. Alone in the evenings, Mother may have grieved, not only for a husband but also for the home she had had, her *own* home, the good modern little house of her married life, which had been succeeded for her by cramming in with the family and then by a series of shabby rented places of which 7 Wolsey Road was by far the best.

* * * * *

There was another way as well in which I felt different at LEHS. I think I thought we were the only poor family. In this I was profoundly mistaken, for there were many other scholarship girls whose families were facing a serious struggle to meet the extra costs of a public school education, but my ignorance was caused by the fact that so little attention was given to a girl's material background. When invited to parties, for instance, I must have seen the comfortable homes that many girls lived in and I would have known that their parents owned cars and other desirable possessions. Yet in school it never mattered in the slightest. Never once, by a single word, did any other child nor any teacher nor other child's parent cast a slur or impute the least suggestion of inferiority. I had no notion whatsoever that such a thing could ever happen, even though our living conditions in the flat were so lowly in comparison with some of theirs.

The same was true in Wolsey Road and there our lives were filled with paradox. We scraped by, counting pennies and shillings down in the half-light where the walls bloomed with dampness and came up to the broad sunlit lawns of the gracious houses all around us. A bus fare had to be reckoned with, while our neighbours drove a Bentley. Disadvantaged and badly off, we attended a public school, while a titled lady scrubbed our floors. It was a marvellous mixture and all to our good fortune, not only from the benefits of being in such surroundings, but also because a diversity of levels in one's background implants an open outlook in one's mind.

* * * * *

There was a great secret in my life at this time and it did not enter my head to tell it to anyone nor even to put it in the Diary. Introverted to the bone, I used to conceal my thoughts quite automatically. When Madame Lécuyer sympathetically tried to find out what was making me worried and sad, and when the envelope incident brought the home background to light, it didn't occur to me to take her at her word and discuss things or volunteer information that might have helped her to know me better. Mummy, of course, would always listen to Jan and me and treat our feelings seriously, yet I shared with her probably fewer than half of all the problems or emotional experiences I went through as a girl. Up to a point I confided in Pamela, and the Diary was an outlet, but neither of these receptacles knew about this particular matter, not the full truth of it anyway. It was all very odd.

It need not have been such a secret. There was nothing very dreadful about it. All it was, was that I was extremely religious.

In the family, as I said in an earlier chapter, there was a variety of beliefs. The strong religious faith of Gagga was juxtaposed to the atheism of my parents. My father's influence had been removed (he had told me when I first went to school that I was *not* to believe what they said about God) and Mother was in truth more an agnostic than an atheist, certainly not antagonistic to religion, but Jan and I had not been christened and she would never have taken us to church.

And so it was at school, at all my schools, that I learned the Bible stories and the prayers, hymns and psalms which other

184

people come by at their Sunday services. By the time I started at Lady Eleanor Holles they were firmly implanted.

LEHS was founded as a Christian school, Church of England in character though not officially, and the Christian teaching that underpinned all its work was revitalised by the deeply religious temperament of Ruth Garwood Scott. By marking the festivals and holy days of the church year more clearly, she introduced elements of a more definitely Anglican flavour where our morning assemblies had previously been of a fairly vague, ecumenical character, but I have no sense of having had religion pushed down our throats.

In any case, it would have been difficult to push any more down my throat, I was so steeped in it already. It may sound sickeningly pious now to say so, but I was truly a devout child, trying to be good and please God, speaking to Jesus in my mind as I walked around and went to lessons. Avidly I soaked up all the history of the Old Testament and the New, and through the year lived and relived the episodes of the life of Christ, especially at Easter and Christmas. Our morning Prayers with which each school day began have left their mark so deep that when I am in my dotage and all other memories have gone, I know the words of hymns will remain to the last.

Christmas above all filled me with awe and wonder, with emotions that choked me. It was holy beyond words. When I was about ten or eleven I had been suddenly struck by the full reality of Jesus' birth. 'In a *stable*' I thought with amazement, 'they were in a *stable*!' – knowing now what a stable was like and seeing the utter lowliness of having to take shelter in such a place and have a baby born in it.

Why these feelings had to be kept so absolutely private I do not know. Perhaps they were not. Perhaps other people saw them perfectly clearly, although I'm not so sure, for there was one person who rather stubbornly did not. This was Auntie Kathleen. Auntie Kathleen insisted that because we three were not churchgoers we could have no religious feelings. The ironic twist here is that on those rare occasions (the details of which will emerge later on) when I did enter a church, it was often with her and she always rather scoffed at the idea that I could

185

possibly have anything to gain from the experience. It was extraordinary that so intelligent a woman could not see beneath the surface. It was not even as if she herself were unquestioningly orthodox, for she once told me that she did not believe in an afterlife and she said that when her daughter, Rosalind, had died, she knew she was never going to see her again.

Gagga used to talk to me about God and Jesus. When the time came for some of the girls at school, including Pamela, to learn their catechism, in readiness for being confirmed, I naturally was not one of them; I was in the group that instead was to study the New Testament, beginning in the summer term of 1950, and Gagga took the moment to hand on to me some of his own thoughts. I remember sitting beside him on the sofa one day, which must have been during the Easter holiday but, sad to say, the only thing I can remember of what he told me was that the Welsh nation is one of the lost tribes of Israel.

In the Diary there are little guarded hints of my faith, benedictions uttered on the deaths of Auntie Margaret and Auntie May – 'God bless her'. And then in the autumn term there came an experimental phase of going public. I think it was through Cynthia that it happened, the girl mentioned earlier with whom Pamela and I now made up a triple friend-ship, for Cynthia was a Baptist and probably, therefore, the instigator. The three of us together decided to join the Chris-tian Union. We went to meetings in the lunch hours. I liked it, but only two meetings are recorded.

In a strange way, it was the beginning of the end. The freethinking, ardently personal form of religion that had devel-oped within me could not 'belong' to anything and as I grew older I ceased to call myself a Christian. All the religions of the world were on an equal footing, I maintained, with none of them holding a monopoly of the truth, and I would embark on a search for God, impelled perhaps by the same need as Gagga. This lay in the future, however, and in the meantime I closed the door and just kept the fire burning quietly within my own hearth.

It was rather on a par with the way my political thought was developing at this time. Apart from whatever I had picked up from the mock election as described in Chapter 2, it was more a case of forming general ideals than learning about party policies or the structure of British government. The greatest single influence on these ideals was the War. Preventing other wars mattered above all else. I was very much a pacifist and opposed to any show of nationalism or patriotism. 'My country right or wrong' seemed to me a terribly narrow and dangerous attitude. I kept my lips clamped shut when the school sang the hymn 'I vow to thee, my country, all earthly things above. . .' and barred myself from joining the Girl Guides because they had to take an oath of allegiance.

* * * * *

Just as there had been a hankering for 'the old summer evenings' back in March, so in the middle of summer I was writing *Another beautiful day. It's rather like a fine Autumn morning when it's early,* and in November *Today was as fine as a spring day!* Perversely out of kilter with whichever season it really was, by 4th September my thoughts had already turned to Christmas. But autumn was truly the favourite.

Sunday September 17 Nice day today. Very windy but sunny. I spent most of morning doing prep. Oh, I've got Autumn in me! The sun was beaming through the carnations in the window and the fire crackled in the clean grate. All so crisp outside. All so cosy inside!

At the age of fourteen I believe I had yet to discover Keats's 'Season of mists and mellow fruitfulness' but it is certain that my sentiments were the same as his on the beauty of autumn. It was the best of the seasons, the golden time of the year, and, above all, it ushered us, with 'the fanfare and the feast of birth', towards the great climax crowning every twelve-month turn of the globe – it brought us up to Christmas.

In 1950 the autumn was less a golden time than a season of wet and dismal chilliness, but it produced its compensations and one of these, on the very day that it officially began, was an evening almost designed as a childhood idyll, a tableau set for nostalgia.

Saturday September 23   Oh, what a wonderful evening! Oh, what a beautiful day! Oh, <u>what</u> a glorious evening . . .!!

Shopping in Kingston together in morning. The shops, especially Woolworths! The decorations, Father Christmas's for sale!

Jenny came round for a while. Tina and the Fermors came later ... Went to play with Tina and made a fire of leaves. After tea, as it got dark, we sat under their garden table on rugs. Cooked some bread which was smashing, sang carols and Mrs. Fermor brought us some orange juice and biscuits.

What can be said about such a very simple, joyous event except that it was the atmosphere that mattered? Camp fires and midnight feasts are not often as thrilling as they are meant to be, but this was one of the rare successes. The building of camps and camp fires had a romantic grip on my imagination, because children seated round a fire had long been a favourite subject for painting, and the adventures of children living in a 'Secret House' in the woods was the theme of an endless story that Jan and I took turns to relate to each other while lying in bed. This gathering, then, was like a story come to life..

Although the repeat performance of the wonderful evening planned for the following weekend was rained off, autumnal ardour was not dampened, and a bonfire one night in our own garden had me in raptures: *Monday October 16 ... Only had one prep! I did a bit of tomorrow's and copied some French verbs up, but at 6.10 I was in the garden. Dusk, a bonfire, Autumn leafy smells and cold air – oh lovely, lovely!*

I appear to have been alone out there on this occasion, alone of the children I mean, and it sounds as though the bonfire was just a gardener's fire lit by Colonel Gettins or Auntie Kathleen rather than one purpose built to attract a circle of bread-baking carol singers. However, it was not long now to Guy Fawkes night. Over at Cambria, still in mid-October, John provided £1's worth of fireworks so that we could have a little early firework party over there with Chris and Steven, Vivien and Adrian; but for the celebration of Firework Night itself I

went to Pamela's. It was more like a whole Firework Weekend.
Friday November 3 Called home to change [after school] *as I'm spending weekend with Pamela. Mummy home in time to say goodbye. Wore best clothes. After tea went in car to Mr. Fish's golf club. Nice firework display there. Pam and I watched T.V. till 9.30.*

Saturday November 4 Had a good pillow-fight this morning. Did some prep ... Then Pam and I had a treasure hunt or two, which we finished after lunch ... went to shops. Saw some children with a lovely big bonfire. Kay, Pam's grown-up cousin came with her 4 year old son, Ian. We had some lovely fireworks. Catherine wheels a failure. Some smashing bangers.

Sunday November 5 Another pillow-fight. Ian helped Pam and I clear up firework remains after breakfast. We found some powder left in some, which we burnt.

So quite a prolonged feature was made out of commemorating the activities of the unlucky Mr Fawkes, although other days of note in the calendar passed by unrecognised. Halloween in its trick-or-treating mode was quite unknown, Mothering Sunday was observed only by the churchgoing community, if at all, and Valentine's Day we might have heard of merely as a custom that once used to give amusement to Victorian young ladies. I doubt if I could have named the dates of any of them. Easter held a prominent place; we gave and received not only Easter eggs but small gifts. Nor was Shrove Tuesday to be missed, although we heathen Applebys, I need hardly say, having shriven ourselves with pancakes made no attempt to undertake any Lenten sacrifices. Christmas, however, towered over all the other festivals and birthdays combined – but the surge of its tidal wave must not carry us forward too fast at this point.

One pleasant by-product of the poor weather was that throughout that year many of our school lunch hours and breaks were spent inside, and as a means of keeping us under control in these circumstances music was provided for dancing in the hall. How the whole senior school could be crowded into the hall and still leave enough space to make up dancing formations, I cannot visualise, but perhaps only a few classes were let in at a time while others remained in their form rooms or sat in the library – I am not sure about this. Anyhow, it was crowded enough, and noisy, but the dancing diminished the risk of our becoming one wild, shouting mob in that confined space. Sometimes there was country dancing, sometimes Scottish and sometimes, to judge from the fact that Pamela once tried to teach me how to waltz, it must have been ballroom. Those who could dance, joined in, and those who could not looked on. *Wet break,* I wrote on 3rd November. *I love sitting in the warm hall watching the dancing and listening to the music. It makes the place seem like a ballroom (though some girls are playing 'He'!),* and an almost identical entry follows for the 28th: *Indoor break. I love to see the dancing and hear the music and noise in the hall. Wish I could dance.*

Wish I could have told somebody that I wished I could dance. But the possibility of telling people about what I felt, desired or disliked seldom crossed my mind, so apart from that effort at the waltz, my wish went unfulfilled.

One *unpleasant* by-product of the weather, indeed of damp autumns in particular, was that in our beloved little flat it brought out the spiders.

Saturday September 16 I saw one spider in bathroom and a huge one in kitchen which Peter [Peter and Joan had come to tea] *killed. I did not have spider-mares though!*

Wolsey Road was the last sort of place in which three arachnophobic females should have been living. The brick-lined areas outside each window, almost as earthy as the soil itself with thick deposits of moss and dead leaves; the ivy growing profusely all over the house; the two cellars described in the first chapter of this book – all these, with the general dampness and vegetable fecundity and the warmth of our basement, made the perfect habitat for a thousand creepy-crawlies.

Mother had realised soon after we moved to the flat the need to block the spiders' pathways into our rooms by stuffing newspaper round the unopened cellar door and into the gaps where water pipes ran through the walls. She had suffered one terrible evening of fear soon after we'd moved in, when one

190

after the other eight of the great, leggy creatures appeared and plopped to the floor before she spotted their point of entry, a jagged hole in the brickwork up in one corner.

All three of us developed habits of spider-wariness, which became second nature to us, as ducking the beams does to those who live in a timbered cottage. We would pull our beds away from the wall each night and see that no covers were left touching the ground. We would never let a dressing gown trail on the floor nor clothes brush against a wall. We often scanned a room rapidly before entering and I tried never to sleep flat on my back in case a spider dropped into my mouth from the ceiling. The one that Peter Green killed for us nearly fooled me though. It was spreadeagled on a dark brown area of wall (there was mock panelling in parts of the flat) and I had gone dangerously close to peer at it before I could tell it was not just an odd mark.

Mother's precautions succeeded in reducing the number of spiders that we actually saw (and that she had to kill), although, of course, we knew they were still around us all the time, but it could not alter their size.

In retrospect, they are something to be proud of. Some of them, had we had the *sang-froid* to preserve them, could have qualified as museum specimens. One above all I shall never forget. It had emerged apparently from the notorious cellar. High up on a cream distempered wall this time it, or *she* no doubt, confronted us and spanned, I swear, the diameter of a saucer. Mother quailed and sent an SOS to the Colonel. Within moments everyone in the house came running down our stairs and stood gazing in awe. Mrs Milton, Auntie Kathleen's housekeeper, was the only one who could handle it and even she, normally quite fearless in such circumstances, had to hold it in a duster.

And not only were they very large, those spiders in our flat. They were creatures of legend. We ought to have been honoured by their presence. 'The common house spider', says the *Oxford English Dictionary* 'sometimes grows to an enormous size and it is then known by the name of the Cardinal Spider'.

No wonder, then, that they were so magnificent. They were Cardinals, they were *the* Cardinal, for the story had it that all Cardinal spiders originated in Hampton Court Palace and with the imprint of the prelate's hat on their backs they were the multiple reincarnations of Wolsey, still weaving possessive webs over his palace. It was from those old Tudor nooks and crannies, therefore, that they had crept and spread, numerous, superior, one of our largest species, the lords of British spiders. So close to their ancestral home, in Wolsey Road no less, they had as good a right as we to be there and for all the shivers down the back they gave us, I see them now as something splendid.

* * * * *

In addition to 'camp-fire Saturday', there were several exciting weekend events in the Autumn of 1950. Two special outings, one of them an impromptu, followed each other nose-to-tail as September gave way to October.

Saturday September 30 ... did some prep before lunch. I planned to have Tina and Jenny in ... However, Mr and Mrs Shepherd asked us to drive down to see Paul with them. It's his birthday and they were taking his presents. What a lovely school! He opened his things in the Matron's room. Paul showed us his dormitry and we saw his friend in the sick room. We all (not Paul) had tea at 'Sally Lunn', a hotel-café. Very nice place. Poor old Paul, not able to come out and have tea with his mother and father and friends at the Sally Lunn on his birthday! But I think that in boarding schools in those days the belief was that the less a child saw of his family and the outside world the better he would settle down.

The outing on the Sunday gave me a final look at the sea for that year. *Pam called with her parents in their car at 9.15.a.m. They're taking me for the day to Hayling Island. Journey took about 1½ hours. Her Granny and Grandad have a dear tiny little bungalow. Strange to say, the place and her Granny reminded me of Nanny's. She has a photo album which plays a tune when opened. We went to their hut on the beach. Pam and I played*

192

ball and other games We also layed lunch in hut for Pam's parents and ourselves. Pam and I read after lunch while grown-ups were out, and we paddled a little. Cold! Back to Granny's for tea then home in the car. Got back at about 7.20.p.m. I have got a bit of a sore throat.

While meeting someone else's granny and grandad, however, it seemed months since we had visited our own. I had stopped briefly at Cambria on the return journey from Southend and there had been those

Hayling Island. Pamela and myself with Mrs Fish and the grandparents

few days Gagga spent in Torquay, but Mummy had not seen her own mother except for one swift teatime visit to Hayes in July. Unfortunately, the LEH half-term did not coincide with that of Molesey Secondary Girls' School for that autumn term and so we could only manage to go for one ordinary mid-term weekend. In any case, Mummy was keeping her week in November free as there had been some plan that she would go down to see Auntie May again. The plan came to nothing in the end, though, because Mummy was far too busy and tired in her first working weeks as a teacher, and Auntie May, former teacher herself, expressed perfect understanding of the difficulties, maintaining the brave fiction that she would be coming to see us instead in the spring when she was better.

Saturday October 21   Finished prep and at 11.0 approx. left

193

for Nan's. Gag met us in the old car. John's here. He's given us £1 worth of fireworks. Saw Julian. He smiled at me!

I drew Steven and we went to see Chris's budgy and goldfish.

John came to Auntie Lizzie and Ettie's with us. Leslie came [a second cousin who lived near the aunts] *and we enjoyed a smashing tea. Auntie Lizzie told us then of the time she was in service in a big house. So interesting! She gave me a scent bottle 100 years old!*

Sunday October 22 Extra hour in bed as clocks were put back. In Nan's bed she told us the old story of the little girl who went to Fairyland. I went down to see Julian bathed and gave him his Farex. Vivien and Adrian came. Vivien goes to a little school now. Played with them. Chris and Steven had lunch with us. All of us children took Julian out in pram. Let off some fireworks after tea. Came home with Viv. and Ad. in car.

So this was the weekend of the fireworks and it was also when Nan gave me her coat. The one hundred year-old scent bottle, now one hundred and fifty, is actually a vinaigrette and hangs on a silver chain originally belonging to a fob watch.

The story of the little girl who went to Fairyland went something like this: a little girl was just about to fall asleep one night when through the window of her bedroom there flew a tiny silver aeroplane. It landed on the windowsill and out got a fairy, who asked the little girl if she would like to go with her to Fairyland. Very surprised, she said yes, she would like to very much, so the fairy made her as small as herself and they flew out of the window together in the tiny plane.

The plane landed and they transferred to a boat in which the fairy rowed the little girl along a river. At last they got to Fairyland and there the little girl met the Fairy Queen and saw all the fairies' pretty little houses and the beautiful tiny flowers everywhere and was given delicious tiny little cakes, tiny apples, tiny bananas to eat and little silver cups of wonderful tasting drinks. At the end of a lovely day, she was brought back in the little aeroplane and woke up in her own bed.

Nan told it all in a whisper, as though not to frighten the fairies, and in a tone of wonderment, describing in far greater detail than I have just done the Liliputian world and its inhabi-

194

tants, demonstrating between thumb and finger the size of the tiny cakes and cups. Her fairies were all of the delicate, gossamer-winged variety, with magic wands; there were no ugly hobgoblins.

It seems rather an oddity on one and the same day to have been given a grown-up coat and to have listened enthralled to a story Jan and I had been hearing since our infancy. But how uncannily symbolic for that year of transition!

* * * * *

Three days after smiling baby Julian had been taken for a walk by all his older cousins, he was dangerously ill in hospital. *Wednesday October 25 Phone call when Mummy came home. Julian has had serious operation! Something got twisted up in him. If it had been found 24 hours later he would have died. Thank God for small mercies!* We were told that the 'twisting' was an intussusception, a sudden telescoping of the intestine, a failing that only boys under two years old were subject to. Within a couple of days Julian was *recovering quite nicely* and he came out of hospital a week later, but to round the story off, since this requires only a small step ahead into 1951, it happened again, more catastrophically, and Julian was within ten minutes of death. Again he pulled through, but a streak of Olwen's hair had turned white.

* * * * *

I never was fully reconciled to having my mother out at work and on evenings when she had to be out late the Diary would always record somewhat possessively the time of her return. I think Jan and I were rather close and clinging children and we missed her. We were glad, therefore, that, now she was teaching, her working day was shorter than at college. *It is nice having Mummy in when we get home!* I wrote. She had marking and preparation to do at home, of course, but at least she was with us.

She was still not as free as she'd have liked, however, and

that term for the first time she had to miss my prize-giving. Faced with a choice as to which of several possible school functions she could attend, and for which of them she would beg an afternoon off, she decided that this time it must be Jan's Prize Day.

It must seem from the Diary that Prize Days, or Speech Days as we sometimes called them, came rather thickly clustered together in 1950, like a convoy of late double-decker buses. It was largely because of the upheaval caused in the school in the previous year by the unforeseen departure of one headmistress and the appointment of Miss Scott in the middle of a term. The result was that the Junior Prize Day due to take place before Christmas 1949 was held in March, as has already been seen, whereas this year's Juniors had caught up again and were able to have theirs in December. The Senior function, for which at long last we young ladies of the Upper Fourth were eligible, was on 30th October.

Our minds were focused upon the great day almost from the beginning of term. The first requirement, as always, was to learn our set songs, and the first reaction on finding out what the set songs were, was to criticise them. *Tuesday September 19 Singing first. Old Scott's decided we can't sing 'Strawberry Fair' on Prize day! The only really nice song we've ever learnt here! All songs have to be by Shakespeare! How thoroughly daft! One wants variety on a Prize day!* Without complaint about such things, life would have hardly been normal; but, fortunately, a swift change of opinion followed. *I like the songs we're singing. We've only three more lessons till Prize day,* I said a week later, and on 10th October *I had to learn another song pretty quickly as I was away last week. It's rather a nice one –* so maybe I had realised that Shakespeare wrote a decent line or two. I know that 'Sigh no more, ladies' was one of those allocated to our form because I used it as the subject of a piece of calligraphy I completed for art homework, and I think the other was 'Where the bee sucks'.

It was Miss Scott, though, more than the Bard, who had been the object of scorn and more disaffection was to come her way. We started rehearsals, consisting of two types – prizewinners-only practices which necessitated arriving early for four mornings and running through the order of presentation before 9.00 a.m., and full rehearsals, when every class involved filed into the hall and ran through the songs and the routine. One afternoon when we were all in there, in order to give the thing the semblance of a dress rehearsal and to help with the timing, I suppose, we were told to applaud the prizewinners as they went up to the platform and our applause developed quite spontaneously into a slow handclap.

Prize rehearsal. We had to applaud prize winners as they went up. Suddenly everyone started clapping in rythm! Miss Scott was furious. I could hardly contain myself. Funniest thing for weeks.

The next day *we had to miss our lunch hour and get lessons finished by 3.0. Miss Scott spoke to us at 3.0 in the hall about Speech Day.* I expect this was a pep talk aiming to eradicate any refractory elements lingering from the day before and put us into the right frame of mind. She was probably strung up with suspense over the success of the event, for it was the proving point at the end of her first year of headship and a very public and exalted occasion, with the Lord Mayor of London as the guest of honour. But *all went well. Lord Mayor of London and sheriffs looked very fine. Our songs were very nice. No-one made a mistake.*

The books I chose as prizes this time were *Wonders of Nature, Velasquez* and *Fra Angelico.*

Mummy had rushed back from school in her lunch hour to help me get ready. *Mummy popped in about 12.30. I had been up to school about 11.30 to collect new school skirt. Mummy did my hair after we both had had a hurried lunch. I dressed carefully in new tie, skirt, etc. Auntie Kathleen ran me to bus stop. Pam met me with her mother. Pity Mummy can't come.*

Prize Day was not only to do with the issue of rewards for good class-work. At a higher level there were the special, named prizes that had been bestowed over the years by governors, benefactors and former headmistresses – prizes for mathematics, history, music, domestic science, languages and one for having shown 'special qualities of character and service to the School'. But above all, it was the time to put before the parents the year's achievements in the public examinations, the grades attained in music, the State Scholarships and bursaries and the places secured in universities, training colleges and medical schools.

Piled up on the table in front of the governors, all those books, certificates and scrolls exemplified the philosophy of the school, which comes back to me now as very robust insistence that intelligence and talent should be used to the utmost.

I cannot remember the value of our education ever being questioned just because we were girls. It was taken entirely for granted. It did not have to be justified or even discussed. We were taught the history of the battle for suffrage and women's rights, but that had taken place some time ago and as far as we

Prize Day 1950. Myself second row from staircase, with plaits. Miss Maden by the piano

198

were concerned the process was complete. This was borne out by the fact that no new term had been coined to describe it. 'Women's liberation', 'women's lib' and then 'feminism' became common currency when the movement started up again, but we still used the same phrase as the Pankhursts did: the Emancipation of Women. Some of the staff, though, I've no doubt, would have been ardent feminists, more conscious than we were of the hard-won fight whose victory we children now thoughtlessly inherited. My mother, too, remembered a time of greater militancy when, for instance, some progressively minded women declined to wear wedding rings, these being symbols of 'bondage'. I'm sure we girls thought that extreme sort of attitude to be no longer necessary. (And female bondage, I need hardly say, did not have the same curious connotations in the 1930s as it would by the '70s or '80s!)

Ex-Lady Eleanor Holles girls entered a great diversity of professions but it was recognised that the majority of us would also become wives and mothers. Miss Scott once said that her chief business was to produce well-educated Christian housewives. Setting aside the 'Christian' epithet as a natural complement, for her, to the main objective, no conflict of interest was implied in this, no 'waste' of a good education suggested. If society as a whole had had the mental breadth and self-assurance that were instilled into us (and that for me prevailed in the family too), there would in the end have been no need for the feminist movement.

* * * * *

Other regular happenings of the autumn term were the Harvest Festival, the Carol Service and the Dramatic Competition.

Wednesday October 11   Colonel let us have some smashing flowers for Harvest Festival. I took a small cabbage and packet of barley corns or something, and flowers to school. Most people had flowers and other things. Jan took some things ... Had a little French, rather a muddled lesson, in p.m. Then service. Very nice. Vicar of Twick. spoke for a change, about St. Francis. All things very nice on platform.

The reason why it was a change to have the vicar of Twickenham to conduct the service was that we usually had the Rev. Everett Turner, vicar of St Giles without Cripplegate, the parish just by the City of London walls where the school had been founded. (This association with the City was also the reason for the Lord Mayor presenting our prizes and for the red cross and the sword of the City arms appearing as they did at that time on our school badge.) Any lone male having to sing in our female congregation would sound out loud and clear, but the Rev. Turner used to give particular delight, confidently booming away at 'Fair waved the golden corn' or 'We plough the fields and scatter' like a bear among chipmunks, his large, bearded figure dwarfing Miss Scott on the platform.

This was not our only opportunity, though, for blending our feminine voices with deeper ones. A Carol Service was held just before Christmas each year in Hampton Parish Church for which we combined with the boys next door, in other words, Hampton Grammar School. Somehow our contact with these boys was always kept to a minimum, even though our grounds and theirs adjoined and were divided by no more than a wire fence, and despite the joint venture of the Carol Service our respective purity was preserved, as there was no danger of the sexes being able to speak to or sit beside one another during this event. The church was a couple of miles from the two schools and we used to go trooping along the Hanworth Road and Hampton High Street in what to onlookers must have appeared an endless line – hundreds of us. On 21st November we *Started practicing in singing for Carol service!! Joy oh, joy for Christmas. We're doing as one of our carols 'Oh, little town of Bethlehem' to a different tune.* But for all our practising, in 1950 the service did not take place. The weather was too bad for the long march.

There was however a Music Club concert on 18th December. *It was jolly good. Some people are jolly good at playing the piano. Some plucky ones sang by themselves. As Miss Scott had told us, we were a sympathetic audience and did not laugh when people made mistakes. We all sang a few carols together.*

A few days previously there had been the Dramatic Competition, in which I played a humble part.

Wednesday November 1   English. Spent almost all time talking about play for dramatic competition. It was quite nice. I want to have some part in it.

Wednesday November 8   I have a backstage part, as I wanted, in our play at school. I'll go to rehearsals, help with costumes, scenery, prompting, etc.

Friday November 24   Rehearsal for play in lunch hour. Hilary and I went to Miss Denney after school and asked if she had any Elizabethan costumes. She will take us under platform one day to sort them out.

Thursday December 14   Dramatic Competition. I was behind the scenes in our play and watching the Lower IV's and V's. It was smashing fun, especially as we won the cup!

How frustrating that the Diary doesn't say what play we did! The only clue is in the quest for Elizabethan costumes. It can't have been anything to do with the 'Slasher Knight' in whose part I was once cast by Miss Duce, as previously mentioned, nor with the Coventry Nativity Play, which we studied at about that time. These seem to have belonged to a weekly drama session in one of our English periods, using the stage in the hall, but they were not part of the Competition, and not always such 'smashing fun'. *Acting in hall in English,* says the Diary. *The first time we do a play we only read it, with readers on platform. It's rather boring.*

Drama as a whole held a prominent place in the school. A class or one of the clubs often put on a little one act play as end of term entertainment, but the major production of the year, with a cast drawn mainly from the Upper Fifth and Sixth forms, came at the very end of the summer term and filled the hall with parents and guests for three highly-charged but joyous evenings. Rehearsals occupied the weeks when these girls at the top of the school floated between the end of the GCE exams and what would be for many of them the final breaking up. It was always a rich period of relative freedom, the burden lifted, results too far away to mind about just yet, a thorough contrast to the weeks of being bowed over examina-

tion papers; an interlude of leisure yet filled with creative, satisfying and refreshing activity.

* * * * *

As at the end of the summer term, some small miscellaneous
items from the Diary, relating to school, home and the world
in general, deserve to be mentioned:

*Friday September 15   Bus strike, so Pam couldn't get to
school. Mummy wouldn't let Jan go in case she couldn't get
home. She has her half day on Friday now so she wouldn't be
able to go with me. I got there on 667* [the trolleybus].

*Tuesday September 26   Total eclipse of moon very early –
3.31 a.m. I didn't watch.*

*Wednesday September 27   Read this morning that there was a
blue moon! Wish I'd seen it. You only get that sort of thing once
in a blue moon!* [Heavy wit]

Thursday September 28   Started winter clothes ...

Friday September 29   [when the Diary had been somewhat
neglected] *So lazy I am! This is being written on 9th October.
No wonder I cannot remember things.*

*Friday October 13   History. Hilary Bowdler, music genius of
our form, gave us a prepared account of music in the Renaissance
...*

*When I took library book back Miss Sturrock was at the desk.
She seemed very pleased I had been reading the 'Book of Art'.*

*Thursday October 26   We have had speeches at Prayers the
last three days about U.N.O. Jolly D.*

*Thursday November 2   Bernard Shaw died in hospital at 5.0
a.m. Aged 94.*

*Friday November 3   History ... interesting lesson. We
discussed B. Shaw and his work.*

*Monday November 6   Only one period of needlework. At 3.0
we went to hall to see some films. There were 3 about life in
Palestine 2,000 years ago. One about a home, one about education, one about the synagogue. They were very realistic, very well
done indeed. The man who showed them came from Bible House.*

Saturday November 11   After lunch we went to a dancing

202

display which some of Mummy's girls were taking part in. Some of it was fair. Most was spoilt by very little girls singing shocking songs. [What on earth can they have been?]

Friday November 17   Went to sign Excellent Book in recess. Quite a lot of others there. I didn't get out at all and didn't eat my lunch. Miss Scott said, when she saw my Latin, 'Yes, very good Madeline.'

Monday November 22   Miss Scott came into English. We were reading a poem about a dog. She rather enjoyed it, I think.

Needlework. I got the back of my blouse machined onto the two bits of the front. I feel I've got on a bit now.

Monday November 27   Shoo's birthday. We left cards and notices.

Monday December 4   French. <u>Lovely</u> lesson (for a change!) Mme. L. has had a new idea that we should have a lesson for discussing something about France every week. Also, she wants Jane Shutes and I to paint the puppet theatre.

In needlework it snowed very hard and settled! I forgot my work and had to practice buttonholes instead.

Friday December 15   Missed English for a book check. Madame Lécuyer handed cumfits round to everybody!! Most startling change has come over her these last two weeks or so!

There is a sad ending to the story of the puppet theatre. It remained unpainted by Jane and me (Jane being another of the leading artistic members of the form), largely because we did not produce a design. The theatre was actually a three-sided wooden structure with a proscenium opening, similar to a Punch and Judy kiosk but of a height suitable to conceal children operating the puppets. It had been painted plain white and we eagerly agreed to brighten it up with colourful motifs. The difficult thing was to think of designs that would convey a theatrical theme without using the traditional tragi-comic masks set among garlands and so forth. My obsession with originality would not allow me to fall back on such a cliché. This silly idea was as if Grinling Gibbons had refused to carve fruit because others had done it before him, but I suppose I was too young to see that the same themes can always be reused in an original way. I think we then toyed with the idea of Pierrot and Pierrette figures, but in a way the same obstacle applied, and what it came down to was that we simply did not get on with it.

Some weeks later Madame confronted us angrily, and quite rightly, for having done nothing, thus adding a little touch of blight to my relationship with her where there had been a chance for it to blossom.

Meanwhile, however, on this side of Christmas harmony still reigned, Madame was in a genial mood, and as we broke up she *shook hands and wished everyone a Happy Xmas.*

Myself with Mme Lécuyer, probably 1952

7

THE LAST DAYS OF THE GANG

Throughout the term, one enterprise had dominated my thoughts more than any other. Regardless of what was happening in school, at home I was planning and organising and producing goods for sale – for The Sale. Even before the end of the summer holiday, plans were building up in my mind: *Monday 4th September I'm <u>terribly</u> excited about sale! Think at the end of this month I'll call a meeting. Got to have extra-super one this time as we did not have one last year.*

The Sale had been created by Jan and me as our own particular extension to Christmas and, like the Gang, it was on childhood's scale a long-standing institution. It had started just before our first Christmas in the flat, Christmas 1946, and it was all due to Auntie Kathleen. She had told us, that year, about the great Christmas tree standing in St Paul's Cathedral around which people could place gifts for the poor and sick children of London. St Paul's was in any case a wonderful cathedral, she said, so perhaps we could find an old toy which we might give to the poor children, and she would take us up there to see it.

Well, we could do better than that.

We decided we would hold a sale and carol concert to raise money and give more to the poor and sick children than we would ever dig out of our own cupboards. We planned that first one all in secret until we were ready to invite our audience, and we broke the news to Mummy one Saturday morning in mid-December that she had better get up early because 'lots of people are coming in here for a sale'. We had painted cards and calendars, made bookmarks and stitched

205

comb cases out of felt. We put up an art exhibition of our drawings and set out our nature table with a display of sea shells, fir cones and dead stag beetles. The visitors were the Gettins and everyone else from upstairs, Mr and Mrs Shepherd and one or two other friends and neighbours. We knew fewer local people then but those who came dug into their pockets benevolently. They paid a threepenny entrance fee to view the displays and were careful not to peek over the screen of chairs until properly admitted. They moved in good order as directed from painting to painting, as though going through a series of rooms in a gallery rather than across about eight feet of dining room. They also bought the cards and calendars and Mummy sold them cups of tea. Then we sang carols to them.

It was an enormous success and made a handsome sum of over a pound, I believe, which Jan and I spent in the nearby toyshop, proud of having something far better than some old cast-off toy to deliver to St Paul's.

We enjoyed the journey to London with Auntie Kathleen. Though she admitted to finding very young children rather tiresome, she was entertaining company for older ones. We went from Hampton Court to Waterloo. I can remember her telling us to listen for a certain porter you could always hear at Earlsfield station, and she mimicked his cockney cry as the train stopped there: a long drawn out 'Erws-feewld!'

When we reached the cathedral we found not one Christmas tree but two, one in the portico, and another inside, with tables beneath its lower branches on which were heaped the donations of the public. Each tree was lit, the outside one glowing against the grey stone in the dank air, the other warm in the hushed vastness of the cathedral. We added our offerings to the pile of toys already there.

It was on this and the subsequent visits that Auntie Kathleen's disapproval of our godless upbringing became apparent. All that I have to go on is a vague impression, but I think what happened was that after we'd left our gifts at the tree she began to lead us round the huge building to see the monuments and the worn old flags hung with honour high above the aisles, the model of the nativity, and the high altar,

206

and that when we had gone some way along the nave she slipped into a pew and knelt to pray. She made it plain that Jan and I were not expected to do the same, indeed, were not *entitled* to do so, for which I'm sure I was only too thankful because I would have found it dreadfully embarrassing. But I am surprised she did not take the opportunity to engender some religious feeling in us, which she must have thought would be a good thing, by encouraging us to participate with her on these occasions.

In the next two years the Sale became a flourishing concern. It was publicised as 'A Sale and Carol Concert in aid of the St Paul's Children's Fund'. On the little clay printing block which I had used for my magazine (see Chapter 5) I rolled off invitations and concert programmes. The concert itself developed into a more sophisticated affair, well-rehearsed, with additional performers from among the friends Jan and I had made since the first Sale, and offering the audience a variety of solos, duets and chorus numbers. Comedy alternated with piety, the singing of 'Good King Wenceslas' in one of our programmes being followed by 'Funny Version of Good King Wenceslas' by P. Shepherd and A Joke by P. Shepherd. When it was his turn, Paul used to bounce through the dining room door (for we all waited backstage in the hall) and rattle off his joke with beaming enjoyment.

'You remind me. Remind you of who? That man. What man? The man you remind me of.' Sometimes he could hardly finish it for laughing, and the audience was usually doubled up with mirth. It took 'Oh, Come, All Ye Faithful' to sober them down again.

Sorrel Fermor recited 'The Goose is Getting Fat' and we all sang 'Away in a Manger'. I made an opening and a closing speech and the finale was 'A March by Everybody' I do not know what I said in those speeches nor why or whither we marched, but when it was done the grown-ups went on enthusiastically to spend their money at the stalls. And what stalls! No use now to try to screen them with chairs. Such lights would not be hid behind 50 bushels. There was still a nature table, of course, but treble its original size, while the art exhibition had waxed three-dimensional, with models of the nativity and of Father Christmas in a sleigh.

A new element entirely was introduced when we applied the principle of audience participation. In addition to raising their voices in the carol choruses, visitors were asked to guess how many peas in a jar, to draw raffle tickets for a cake and to have their fortunes told. On every table, our ashtray tills filled up with cash and as the guests left they generally tipped much of their remaining small change into them.

No wonder that by 1950 there was a feeling of a great tradition to live up to and the need for a feast of native handiwork to be produced. True to my intentions, therefore, I did hold a meeting later in September, and in fact it was that meeting bringing Jenny Bellears, the Fermors and Jan and me all together for the afternoon which ended in the glorious gathering round the campfire.

The following day we started making things. *Sunday September 24 Very wet day ... Spent most of day making Christmas things, doing homework and reading. Jan and I have got several candles done with Tina's help, a few cards and calenders, purses, etc., from last year.*

What had happened to the 1949 Sale I cannot tell you, but the existence of those unused goods shows that we had abandoned it after starting the preparations, and I cannot help feeling that the 1950 event nearly came to nothing too. The whole of October passed without further meetings and with no mention of making any more candles or calendars, and when at last Jan and I did come together again with the other girls, we had reached a slightly disappointing but practical decision.

Sunday November 12 Jan and I started on Sale work and then Tina came! She had some painted jars and a beautiful apron she had made for a raffle. We have finally decided to have no play, puppet show or concert, but a plain sale. We made lots of cards and labels and Tina came again after lunch and got on making a peg-bag.

At least, then, all our efforts were to be concentrated in the one direction, and with only three weeks to go, for 2nd December was the date booked, there was hardly a chance to do otherwise. We might also have been considering the fact that Paul had left a gap by going off to boarding school, making himself unavailable to be our stand-up comedian.

Tina Fermor used to produce some of the most genuinely useful and attractive articles put on sale. I don't remember how she made the candles, but she was an exceedingly good needlewoman and in working at any craft was skilled and careful. I must admit that my work by comparison tended to be a little slapdash and, because I had always been praised and encouraged to think of myself as artistically talented, there was a tinge of complacency in my attitude, an idea that anything I made or painted would be greeted by adults with adulation. As we grew older, however, our standards of manufacture must have improved all round.

Those industrious hours were very satisfying. Snuggled into the flat like beavers, we would sit round the dining room table, busy and engrossed, surrounded by coloured paper and poster paints, ribbon, tape, fabric, scissors, embroidery silks, silver glitter, pots, jam jars and cardboard. We all wove mats and baskets in raffia and cane, gilded fir-cones and made paper decorations. We used a type of gloss paint which we called 'glass paint' to decorate empty jam jars and turn them into flower vases. It came in tiny cans and in very pleasing colours and we could buy it from Usher's, the ironmongers in Bridge Road. Plastic plates, napkin rings and combs were similarly made splendid with colour and design. We must have spent a good deal of money on our raw materials.

Three weeks to Sale! I exclaimed on 18th November, but in fact it was only two. *Spent afternoon fiddling around mostly with sale things ... I made two telephone books.* And then on the Sunday: *Jennifer did not come to-day and talk over Sale as I had hoped she would. Jan and I made some things but not many.* Somehow the impetus was slowing down and I sense that the other girls were weary of the demands I made on them and the assumption that they would be as keen as I was; but I daresay it was too late by then to cancel the thing, and I had to chivvy them into seeing it through to the end. On Friday 1st December in the evening *I went to see Jenny and Tina about last plans. Was late to bed making notices and getting things together.*

But when the great day came at last, for me at any rate its spirit had revived.

Saturday December 2 This day which I have longed for is come! The Sale! Usual bustle in morning. Cleared dining room, rearranged it. Jan got nature things from garden, set them up on board. I did the table with blue crepe paper, cotton wool and all things set out.

Tina took over raffles, Jan was gypsy fortune teller. 10 people came, bought nearly everything. Sonja and Patsy came. Pam called in. We collected £2. 6s. 8½d. Joan, Peter, Mrs Pern told us about their past Christmases. They stayed to tea.

Jan's fortune telling was popular. She was dressed in a yellow gypsy bandeau and sat in a corner with a tape measure, measuring people's necks and wrists and reading off their luck from the reverse side of the tape measure. To Jenny's mother, Mrs Bellears: 'Too fat to love' and to Colonel Gettins: 'You are a nice one to meet in the dark'. Nearly as good as Paul's jokes.

Sunday December 3 Yesterday was a wonderful day!

Did prep in morning and helped Auntie Kathline with her Christmas pudding. It was fun weighing things and mixing them up. I feel Christmas is really coming now the sale is over and Christmas puddings are being made.

It was not really over, though, not entirely over, until we had bought the toys and taken them to St Paul's. This had to wait until we had broken up for the Christmas holiday and by then the takings had mysteriously been rounded up to three pounds ten shillings.

Thursday December 21 I went out in morning to get gifts with the Sale money. I didn't realise that £3.10s could be so difficult to spend! I bought toys of all kinds for children of all ages and still had 16/4d left!

After lunch Auntie Kathleen and I went to London to Saint Paul's. We put the presents on the Christmas tree which looked beautiful. We looked all round the Cathedral, saw the Crib put up. We went to Auntie Kathleen's flat for tea, then went to

210

Trafalgar Square but the tree there was not lit up. Our good deed is over for this year. Happy Xmas to all poor and sick children! To think we have helped about 20 or more!

Jan had evidently declined the opportunity of another trip to London in Auntie Kathleen's company, and so it was left to me to deliver what would be our final charitable offering to St Paul's. For though it sounds from the passage above as though we anticipated future Sales, there were to be no more. The peak was passed. Perhaps even Jan could not quite share the rapture that had driven me into it, and 1950 was the last year of the Sale.

* * * * *

Friday November 10 [second day of our half-term] *To-day <u>has</u> been a lovely day! Jan and I painted little Christmas cards till after Shoo came. About 11.0 we went off to Kingston. We went to Bentalls, saw Father Christmas, got a present from him. Met Pam there and saw several of our school girls, looked round the shop. I went, when we came back, straight to Woolworth's.* [This must mean Woolworth's in Molesey.] *Bought two more gifts, some wrapping paper, fancy boxes and a card for Pamela. I brought fish-and-chips back for lunch.*

All afternoon we made cards, labels, etc. We did small cards, some of which I'll give to school friends.

Last evening I spent 2½ hours at the piano, learning carols. I did some more this evening.

Monday November 13 In exactly 6 weeks it will be Christmas Day!

Friday November 24 Christmas Eve in 1 month to-day!

Saturday November 25 Bought first tangerines to-day. They smell 'Christmassy'!

Saturday December 9 Christmas shopping in Kingston. Went round Bentalls, Woolworths and Cuffs. Got a lot of gifts. It was terrificly crowded.

Sunday December 10 Wrapping parcels to-day. I painted labels and wrapped gifts in crèpe paper or coloured boxes with bows or Xmas string round. They take a long time. I did not mind.

211

Monday December 11   We had first carol singers this evening.

If you are beginning to think that, with the Sale, there has been enough of Christmas, then let me warn you that the Diary is relentless. These entries are quite separate from the Sale, and show that there was much, much more on the same topic.

By far the greatest part of our activities was to do with giving presents: choosing them, buying them, making some of them, wrapping them and, where relevant, posting them. The astonishing thing is that we not only gave some small object to every member of the family and to many friends, including Joan and Peter, Barney and Bart and their children and undoubtedly Auntie Kathleen, but that to many of these people, Mother, Jan and I gave separately. *Got a present for Oly. I have three gifts ready now,* I wrote in October, clearly implying that I was buying solely on my own account and not jointly with Mummy and Jan. Between us, we must have processed scores of inexpensive trinkets and trifles.

We epitomised to a high degree that aspect of Christmas always so roundly condemned by purists, the commercial side of it. Yet somehow, by our reverence for every detail, the tying of every ribbon, the colour scheme of every label, we made it sacred. Jan and I entered into the spirit of the season with an almost swooning passion, observing all its annual occurrences, like the arrival of tangerines, as precious rites, and when the excitement was too much for any other outlet we would utter our 'joy shriek', a high, prolonged, throaty squeal of ecstasy.

Strange to say, some of the rituals that other families would consider crucial to Christmas were not part of our tradition. We may have had fun helping Auntie Kathleen to mix puddings, but we never mixed our own. We did not send letters up the chimney to Santa Claus. We did not go to midnight mass, we did not have friends in for drinks, we did not make a grand event out of Christmas Eve supper.

This is not to say we kept no rituals. On the contrary, it must be easy to see that we were sticklers for ritual, and the procedures for Christmas Day and Boxing Day were laid down as though they were the law of the land.

212

There were rituals at school as well as at home. We decorated the form room and about a week before breaking up some volunteer would come trundling in with an old cardboard box that she had covered with red crêpe paper and probably topped with a layer of cotton wool snow. The box would be perched on the shelf and we would post cards to one another into the slit in its side. Luckily, we did not exchange gifts with school friends in anything like the same quantities as in the family, indeed it was against the school rules to bring presents for either mistresses or girls; Pamela was the only person there for whom I bought a present. Cards were different, though. *When we opened our post box yesterday,* I wrote, *I'd got 32.* This must represent one from every classmate and one from Madame Lécuyer. I think nearly everybody in the form gave a card to everybody else.

Despite the numerous shopping trips and the time spent in choosing gifts, very little is said in the Diary as to what the gifts actually were. There is only one excursion that specifies a few of the things we bought. It was on the first day of the Christmas holiday. *It's good to be home. Mummy is still at school. I went to Kingston to buy Pamela's gift in afternoon. Shoo and Jan decided to come. I also got an adress book for Mummy, some balloons and little toilet bags to give to various people. We watched in Bentall's window a story told by a series of moving models. It's very pretty and cleverly done.*

This entry still does not say who were the 'various people' destined to receive little toilet bags, nor does it tell me what I bought for Pamela, even though on our way to school the day before I had opened the present she had got for me, and it was *A wonderful box of poster paints!* I hope I gave her something equally suited and well-chosen, because those poster paints were with me for many years and I remember my pleasure on first looking at them.

I cannot pretend that we children gave no thought, as Christmas grew nearer and nearer, to what we would get as well as what we were giving, but thinking and guessing were all we could do about the matter. Our opinions were not sought. We were not asked what we would like nor told how much

213

would be spent on us. Presents were hidden from us, enfolded in secrecy, and the magical thrill of Christmas Day lay in the unwrapping of surprises.

Some of them remain a secret because I do not know either what Mummy gave to me or what Jan and I gave to each other.

* * * * *

And so at long last we came to the great festival itself.

The period of time we spent at Cambria made up the Six Days of Christmas.

Saturday December 23 We have decided Jan and I shall go to Nanny's this afternoon instead of tomorrow.

Mummy was cooking most of the day, mince pies, flans, a sponge, etc. I wrapped parcels as fast as possible. I've got more than I thought I had. Jan and I reached Nan's at about 5.0. Gag could not meet us as his car has broken down.

Sunday December 24 Christmas Eve! As car is broken down I went to Southall with Chris, instead of Gagga. We collected and gave gifts and wished Aunties all the best. Mummy, John and Shoo arrived. We decorated room with balloons, paper things, etc. Xmas tree looks smashing! We set eatables on cabinet and piano.

Hung our stocking up ...

It is almost certain that Chris and I would have collected from Auntie Lizzie and Auntie Ettie not only gifts to bring back but Christmas puddings as well and the chief reason why we did not need to make any of our own was that Auntie Lizzie made them for everyone.

Hanging the decorations required artistic care, in order that the garlands should drape from the centre of the ceiling to the corners in precisely symmetrical loops and the balloons should be tied in harmoniously matching bunches. It was all directed therefore by somebody who took a very long time to do it and who was rather a fanatical perfectionist about the little details. She could call upon Uncle John if need be to push in the drawing pins in the highest places.

The 'eatables' that were set out consisted of sweets and fruit. It was one of the festive customs that on Christmas Day and Boxing Day we were allowed to eat whatever we wished from these bowls all day long, so they would be rummaged at an early stage in the celebrations, but for Christmas Eve they remained scrupulously untouched, arranged to please the eye before the stomach.

And then we hung our stockings up. This for Jan and me was one of the supreme moments of Christmas. We would go up to bed together singing 'Jingle Bells', not of course that Americanised version with its one-horse open sleigh, but the original English children's song about climbing the stair, nodding sleepy head, hanging stockings in a row and hearing the jingle bells of Santa Claus' sleigh very softly from a distance at first, building up to the crescendo of 'here comes good old Santa Claus, arrived on Christmas Day!'

Monday December 25   Day began at 6.50. a.m. Christmas Day began!

Jan and I opened stockings. Lovely things inside! Flannel, soap, calender, pencil sharpener, lots of things to eat, a HUGE orange.

After breakfast, when everyone had washed, we opened other gifts. 'Oxford Book of English Verse' from Gagga. Chocolates, another book, money, Nan and John gifts, a stationery set and Biro from Aunties Lizzie and Ettie.

Lunch was very late, but Boy! was that turkey worth waiting for!! Lots of crackers! We had a quiet afternoon though a short one. We had a small tea. I had a bit of cake for the sake of the icing. Ordinary bedtime tonight. I've been eating almost all day.

It's over now. Oh, how happy I've been!

Christmas Day was supposed to be quiet and peaceful. It revolved around the handing out of presents and the serving of lunch. The adults expected to be able to sit back and rest once the main meal was over, while the children played quietly with their new toys or looked at their new books.

It seems that we were not a particularly large number round the table that day. I think there were only we three, Nanny and Gagga, John and Shoo. Where Shoo would have

215

been sleeping I cannot imagine, but she must have had the privilege of being the only person outside the family ever to have been included in our Christmas household. Olwen and Yoka with the boys nearly always walked over to Yoka's people in Cowley, three or four miles away, and they must have spent both Christmas Day and Boxing Day there, as there is no mention of them in the Diary for those two days, though I daresay we saw them in the morning before they set off. As for Uncle Mansell and Auntie Kitty, they had gone abroad, I believe, and so for once they were missing from the scene. Uncle Ken and Auntie Barbara joined us on Boxing Day.

It is rather odd that Christmas lunch should have been acclaimed so heartily in the Diary because on reflection I realise that Jan and I ate scarcely fifty per cent of the standard fare. For one thing, Jan did not even eat turkey. Her Christmas dinner used to consist of chipolatas and mash. We both hated the sprouts, and as for pudding, despite the fun we'd had weighing and mixing with Auntie Kathleen, we would hardly dream of consuming it! Anything so dark and fruity was far too nasty and bitter, and the same went for the Christmas cake. I might go so far as to have a mince pie but I very much disliked the hard bits of candied peel that one came across inside it. Brandy butter would have made a difference, for I cannot imagine not liking this at any age, but we never saw it in my childhood. I believe that fresh cream was served with the pudding and pies, and this was still a great luxury, since without refrigerators it was so hard to keep, but I know I preferred my good old 'Libby's', the evaporated milk dubbed with its brand name. My tastes were very plebeian. When it came to the drink, Jan and I were allowed a sip of wine but, as with all the more rich and sophisticated foods, I failed to understand how the grown-ups could really enjoy it and was convinced that for my own palate it would never replace lemonade and Tizer.

Tuesday December 26   Gagga took me to the hospital this morning. Matron remembered me from last year. [That was when we had gone to see Auntie Margaret.] *I played the piano*

216

to her a bit. She gave me a drink and biscuit. John and Jan came down and Ken picked us up in his car to go home.

Vivien, Adrian and Auntie Barbara there. They opened the gifts all over sitting room floor. What a shambles! But what fun.

Real fun and games started in evening. V. and A. stayed up till about 7.30. We stayed up till about 11.30. We had some smashing games. Guessing games, singing, and gifts off the Xmas tree! Nanny was good and nearly beat us all once!

The character of Boxing Day was more boisterous and noisy than Christmas Day. The right to eat without asking first continued, and we children were granted our second freedom which was to stay up until we were drooping and dropping asleep on our feet.

My mother used to love the old games. She liked to think that Oranges and Lemons, Nuts in May and My Mother went to Paris were being kept alive by us and handed on from one generation to another. Monkey Motion was another favourite. Her chief role for the evening would be with John as her accomplice in the practice of Black Magic. This guessing game, so simple when you know its secret, kept Jan and me mystified for many years.

Between or after the games, singing was enshrined as a family tradition. We all sang well and could harmonise naturally. The communal Welsh soul leapt into life. Usually, Ken and Mansell would do their party pieces from Gilbert and Sullivan, and then everyone would go rollicking through 'One Man Went to Mow' or 'In Dublin's Fair City'. Without Mansell, the party must have been a little thin in 1950.

Then it would be Gagga's turn, not to sing but to recite. He had to give us 'The Boy Stood on the Burning Deck', or at any rate his own famous rendering of it, for which he took on the character of a small boy supposedly reciting the verses at a concert and forgetting the words. The boy begins confidently, announcing the title, *'Casabianca'* in grand style. But soon he comes to a halt, begins again and repeatedly gets stuck at the third or fourth line. Gradually he breaks down, trying not to cry but finally bursting into tears though refusing to give up. By the end of the act Gagga would be rubbing his eyes with his fists and howling out the words between great heaving sobs, while the rest of us applauded joyously at the familiar performance.

But where we really came into our own was in the hymn singing. It must have dated from the childhood chapel days of the Jones brothers and sisters. Two hymns belonged especially in our repertoire, one majestic, one sombre, and neither having anything to do with Christmas – 'Bread of Heaven' and 'The Old Rugged Cross'.

The 'Old Rugged Cross' was more or less a family anthem. We sang unaccompanied. There was a piano in the room, and I suppose John could have played, but standing round in a group that represented almost the full compass of the human voice, we needed no backing to form a rich and sonorous choir.

There, then, is another sound to rise and fade away down the years within the walls of Cambria –

> So I'll cling to the old rugged cross
> Till my burden of sin I lay down,
> Yes, I'll cling to the old rugged cross
> And exchange it some day for a crown

And with that, we need a last cup of tea and a turkey sandwich before we go quietly upstairs, remembering not to wake Vivien and Adrian, although they have slept through the singing so there is no great risk.

Christmas, that I have longed for since the summer, is gone!

* * * * *

Wednesday December 27 Gagga is not well and is not going to Torquay with Mummy as planned.

Thursday December 28 Gagga still not well so alas, we went home. We'll come back on Monday for Mummy to go to Torquay. Mummy went home in morning but Shoo, Jan and I went after lunch. Helped Nanny, played cowboys with Chris and Steven.

And with these words we have come to the end of the story. The entries in the Diary for the last three days of the year are sparse, separated by large gaps, broken by an unfinished sentence, and even showing on 30th December, for the one and only time in the book, an entirely blank page. So the threads are best drawn together and tied off here as we go home from Nan's.

That happy Christmas Day and the Boxing Night revels had been bought for us children at some cost. As they so often had to do, the adults succeeded in shielding us from worry and sorrow. They hid their true feelings. It seems that I was quite thoughtless of what Gagga might be suffering that year. He had buried the last of his brothers and sisters only a few days beforehand, yet I have no memory of wondering whether he was sad, nor of showing him any special sympathy. I can only hope that as he and I walked together to Hayes Cottage Hospital I talked to him about Auntie Margaret and Auntie May.

Mummy too must have felt for the loss of Auntie May and she hated the thought of having to go to Torquay on her own. Without Gagga, the long journey would be twice as wearying and the winding up of Auntie May's affairs twice as difficult. It was a sad and heavy task.

How far Gagga himself, or Mother standing in for him, was responsible for the sale of Woodstock and the disposal of its contents I do not know. I believe that under Uncle Alfred's will, May had only a life interest in the property and that on her death it reverted to the Harris family. All that came to the Joneses were a few personal effects.

But besides this burden, it also seems clear now, from reading that Gagga became unwell as soon as the celebrations were over, that he had felt ill all along. The illness was spoken of to begin with as 'gastric flu' and there was the additional fact that as long ago as September *Mummy took me to a mass X-ray place, as Gagga had a TB. spot.* But the spot on the lung was a red herring (it didn't develop) and the gastric flu was a euphemism. Gagga had cancer. None of us knew this for a while, although I think he himself guessed the truth at an early stage. He was to die within four months.

And so 1950 ends on a melancholy note.

It had been a year which in retrospect can be seen to contain two strong threads, one from the past and one leading into the future. You might say that any year from anybody's life is a progress between the past and the future but there are not always such a clear-cut ending of one aspect and starting of another, overlapping as they do here. Our future in 1950 was signposted by the beginning of Mother's life as a teacher, while the element from the past drawing to a close was of course my childhood, symbolised by the dying away of the Gang. This vital feature of our lives came to an end within the final pages of the Diary, for that game of cowboys with Chris and Steven just before we went home from Hayes marked out the 28th December, without our knowing it, as the very last day of the Gang.

DEDICATION

No dedication was given at the beginning of this book. It is given now, and the dedication is of course to my mother, the Mummy of the Diary, who died in 1994 at the age of seventy nine. If you go to Hampton Court Palace you will find a seat named in her memory in the Wilderness. She continued to teach in Molesey for twenty six years. She bought the home she wanted, and there *was* a 'golden age'.

Christian Based Cognitive Behavioural Therapy

How to Become Mindful of Christ

Written by
Lauren Roskilly

Lauren Roskilly